SCULPTRESS
FORGOTTEN

© 2021 Gay Bondurant

Suggested retail price.

US: $9.50

UK: £6.99

EU: €7.87

SCULPTRESS FORGOTTEN

ART, THE GREAT DEPRESSION AND THE TUMULTOUS LIFE OF JOAN KELLER

By John R. Allen, Jr

New, expanded, second edition.

John R. Allen, Jr.,
Introduction by Malcolm Lauredo, Director of Historic
Research
In Association with Orestes Gonzalez
© CORAL GABLES MUSEUM, Second Edition, 2021

Cover design based on an original drawing of Keller's two
sculpted firemen by Gay Bondurant, a Museum volunteer
guide, and long-term Coral Gables resident.

ISBN: 9781727093711

JOAN KELLER

TABLE OF CONTENTS

INTRODUCTION

When I started working at the Coral Gables Museum in the Fall of 2016, Joan Keller was the name on a plaque below a photograph in a gallery hallway that bore more questions than it did answers. The photograph captured a young woman standing next to a pedestal on which a half-finished, yet highly detailed sculpture rested. The subject of the picture, Ms. Keller, was being watched by a surrounding crowd of men and women in what appears to be bustling art convention somewhere in Hollywood, FL. The plaque below the photo briefly described a young woman who was trained by the Federal Art Project, a WPA arts education program enacted during the Great Depression. The dialogue card ended with the enigmatic line "What became of Joan Keller after the New Deal era is a mystery."

The Coral Gables Museum, which was built in 1939 and was originally used as Coral Gables' Police and Fire Station, is now home to exhibits, curators, historians, and museum patrons alike. The longer I worked at the Museum, the more I found myself enamored with the dead-pan beauty of the building that housed it. The coral, the courtyard, the tower, and most importantly, the winding history of the structure were always in my peripheries as I carried out my daily tasks. For whatever reason, however, I rarely found myself on the west side of the building - until I finally did. A small deviation in my daily routine brought me to "The Firemen." I found myself at what once was the firetruck bay doors, looking up, and feeling a little smaller than I had a few moments before.

As my head was tilted backward and my eyes were aimed upwards, I saw a community. I saw men, women, boys, and girls. I saw a jester and I saw animals, dogs, cats and birds. They had smiles on their faces and wore a care-free demeaner. Yet, they all looked so small and vulnerable. Disaster and misfortune are always lying-in wait and people tend to forget how fickle good fortune can be. In front of this collective of care-free persons are the firemen. The larger-than-life coral busts of these fire fighters are situated front and center, bearing the brunt of disaster and danger, much like a concrete dam protecting a city from imminent destruction.

It was then that the mystery truly became mysterious to me. Mysteries are meant to be solved, and I am forever grateful to have watched John Allen and Orestes Gonzalez unearth the answers. It was in the wake of this research project that the Coral Gables Museum's Historical Research Division was born, a department I was lucky enough to be chosen to direct. This publication, "Sculptress Forgotten: The Life and Times of Joan Keller", is our department's first venture and is the epitome of what our Historic Research Division stands for: "To pursue and preserve the history of Coral Gables before it is forgotten and lost."

This project was nothing but a labor of love. Love for somebody who died a long time ago and for somebody whom John and Orestes will never meet. And labor is an understatement. I watched them put their lives on hold to breathe life into somebody who had long since passed away. I would often ask them what they would be doing after work and was frequently met with the response "I've got a date with Joan." Funny enough, it is as if you, the reader, now have a date with Joan as well.

Her story is both beautiful and tragic. It is a stark reminder that accomplishment and life's sadness's often go hand in hand. Whether it's a collapsing building or a moment in the spotlight, a knife fight or a coral fountain in an elementary school, a drunk driver or the comfort of family, it's all life. Joan was an artist. She sculpted, shaped, and observed. History is an art form as well. It's the art of remembering.

Malcolm Anthony Lauredo

May 2018

JOAN KELLER

On a quiet Sunday afternoon nearly 80 years after the completion of the Municipal Building, by then the Coral Gables Museum, Orestes Gonzalez, a 21-year-old staff member as well as a budding historian, was lightheartedly challenged by the Museum's director to see if he could uncover any new information on Joan Keller and what had become of her. It was unlikely she would still be alive at the age of 102. Beside the sculptures on the Museum's exterior, had other pieces of her work, which was known to encompass several mediums, survived the intervening 80 years? Had she married and retired from the art world? Did she have children? As Gonzalez waded through dozens of websites, newspapers and ephemera, the questions multiplied far quicker than possible answers, and then every answer, more likely than not, prompt yet more questions. Gonzalez was faced with a series of dead ends, wrong identities, innuendos and rumors. For every fact, there was a counter rumor, for every detail and each tempting nugget of truth, there were misleading, hazy statements and, more often than not, complete fiction. Slowly, after long months of research, the fragmented pieces of Keller's life began to come together. Then Gonzalez finally got the big break he needed to solve the enigma of Joan Keller when he located and connected with her closest living relatives. These were people who had known the elusive woman well and who gladly helped him fill in several of what until then had remained frustrating question marks. A bonus was that several of them lived less than 10 miles from the Museum. When a meeting with family members took place at the Museum soon thereafter, one of her nephews was asked to describe his aunt. He paused only briefly before replying that "Tess" (as she was known in the family) was, "beautiful, talented and a non-conformist." What follows is the fascinating story of the short, tragic, and talented life of the remarkable Joan Keller.

CHAPTER I:
CORAL GABLES,
FLORIDA, 1937

CORAL GABLES, FL, 1937

Like the rest of the United States, the young city of Coral Gables was still mired in the quagmire of the Great Depression. Nationwide, millions remained unemployed, while for many breadlines and soup kitchens had become a part of the normal way of survival. Although signs of recovery had begun in 1933, unemployment was still at 25% four years later, and would still be at a dismal 15% as late as 1940. To stimulate a quicker recovery, in May 1935, two years after being elected President, Franklin Roosevelt issued an Executive Order creating the Works Progress Administration (WPA) to increase employment and lessen direct relief assistance.

With Harry Hopkins, a confidante and close advisor to the President, at the helm, the WPA, and its several divisions, was the largest and most ambitious of the "New Deal" agencies. Between 1935 and 1943, it employed 8.5 million people – primarily men – to carry out not only public works projects, but to also include assistance for education projects, literacy programs, builders, artists, writers, media personnel, the performance arts and other fields. Instead of direct relief assistance, Hopkins and Roosevelt agreed that the most effective way to economic recovery would be by putting people back to work. Three decades later, Hallie Flanagan, national director of the Federal Theatre Project, recalled that "for the first time in the relief experiments of this country the preservation of the skill of the worker, and hence the preservation of his self-respect, became important."

During the eight years of its existence, almost every community across the country would have a new bridge, a park, a school, a public building, or other improvements constructed by the WPA. This included the young City of Coral Gables, incorporated in 1925 and the masterpiece of the creative and passionate visionary and founder, George E. Merrick. In the wake of the Florida Land Bust, Merrick had ben unceremoniously ousted from the Commission of the city he created.

It is interesting to note that the formerly self-imposed banishment of Merrick ended in 1935, when the Florida governor appointed him to the state-mandated Dade County Planning Board, to which he devoted an enormous amount of time, and was soon appointed Chairman. By law, the Planning Board had to approve Depression-era projects built by the WPA, the Civil Conservation Corps, and the Public Works Administration. Under his leadership, Coral Gables received approval for a new Library/Woman's Club, an expanded Coral Way and the new Municipal Building. Truly in his element when addressing an audience, Merrick was a popular speaker at national conferences, and soon was also elected Chairman of the new Dade County Zoning Board. Sadly, due to heated conflicts with politicians and other bodies, he quit in disgust in 1938. By then, however, the new Municipal Building had already broken ground.

The previous year, In November 1937, the City Manager E.M. Williams advised the Chamber of Commerce that the City had applied to the WPA for $116,000 in the construction of a new *"city hall and police station."* Initial plans had been drawn up, and working plans were already in the hands of the architects. The city was to provide the land, situated on the northeast corner of Aragon Avenue and Salzedo Street. Across the street, on the northwest corner, was the popular Coral Gables Riding Academy and Ring. Chamber President W. Keith Phillips related that new building, keeping with the materials preferred by George Merrick, would be built from "quarry key stone." The new edifice would replace the existing police station, located at the corner of Salzedo and Alcazar, three blocks north of Aragon and would be just a block from the heart of Coral Way's business district on Coral Way (three blocks of which would later be known as the iconic Miracle Mile.)

With construction now a certainty, shortly thereafter a young WPA artist, using, as legend would have it, the name John Keller, secured the commission for creating and executing the decorative carvings, or at least many of them, for the building's façades. The most important would be a pair of oversized chiseled heads of two helmeted firemen hewn from coral rock. Many of these works were symbolic - some subtly so, others, such as the firemen, more obvious. John Keller, if that was in fact the name the artist used when applying for the commission, was, for reasons we shall see, not the artist's actual given name. In truth, the sculptor was a 21-year-old woman named Theresa Ida Keller. Sometime prior to 1937, Theresa had dropped her given names and had adopted the name Joan Keller. To further complicate matters, she would also later use a confounding number of other aliases, most notably Jon Keller, an obvious variation of her father and brother's given name of John. The keystone firemen sculptures would eventually become one of the Coral Gables' most iconic images. Keller's career would move quickly from success to success until a serious accident broke her back, nearly killing her only three years later.

After that critical setback, the trail of Joan Keller began to move from hot to warm, then from cool to cold. While some facts and newspaper articles continued to emerge, they soon dwindled - a brief aside here, a passing mention there. By the 1970s, no one seemed to know what had become of one of the most promising artists of her generation. In 1975, the Municipal Building, where her work had launched her career, was replaced by a new municipal complex a few blocks south. For the following 30 years the distinctive Depression era building was used for local government offices and retail space.

Commencing in 1994, a coalition of citizens and local organizations, admirably led by City Commissioner Wayne E. "Chip" Withers began the long process of transforming the historic building into a civic museum that would showcase local history and serve as a community center. As a child, Withers would watch the fire hoses being hung in the building's tower to dry after being used. By 2007, thanks in large part to Withers' persistence, the extensive restoration and enlargement of the building was underway. It officially culminated on October 10, 2010, with the official opening of the Coral Gables Museum.

Along the wall of one of the photo galleries there is an interesting shot of Joan in 1938, looking no older than a teenager (she was 22), demonstrating her skills before an engaged audience at a convention in Hollywood, FL. The small plaque below the photo read *"Whatever Became of Joan Keller after the New Deal Era is a mystery."* Over the decade that followed, scores of visitors and Museum staff, puzzled over that enigmatic, brief text. What had become of Joan Keller? It seemed no one knew, or frankly considered it important enough to merit much thought.

SCULPTRESS FORGOTTEN

CHAPTER 2

BEGININGS IN CLEVELAND, 1916-1935

BEGINNINGS IN CLEVELAND, 1916-1935

Theresa Ida "Tess" Keller was born in Cleveland, Ohio on November 30, 1916, the third child of John August and Marie Frances Roach Keller. John Keller was a first-generation American, born in Erie, PA on May 13, 1891. He was one of at least seven children of August Keller (1864-1925, possibly anglicized from Koeller,and Ida Diemer (1864-1925), both natives of Germany. August had emigrated from Germany in 1885, and married Ida in 1889. The 1900 census shows August and Ida living at 642 South Morgan Street, in Chicago's 8th Ward. August apparently had at least some education, as he could read, write and speak English, and was variously employed as a piano finisher and a meat salesman.

John August Keller

John Keller's wife, Marie Frances Roach was born on August 8, 1894, the daughter, and apparently only child, of Michael Francis Roach (1865-1939, a native of Cleveland, son of Patrick Roach and Elizabeth Harris) and Julia Mary Nicholson. Marie was the granddaughter of Irish immigrants on both sides. Julia Mary predeceased her husband, but details are lacking on her dates of birth and death. Michael's death

Marie Roach Keller

notice stated he was the husband of the late Mary Roach, the father of Mrs. Marie Keller, and the grandfather of Julia, John, Theresa, and Margaret. The obituary overlooked the fact that Marie was legally not Marie Keller, but the widowed Mrs. Marie Bernier.

Marie Roach was 17 and John Keller was 21 when they married in Cleveland April 17, 1912, two days after the world was stunned by the sinking of the Titanic. At the time, John was employed as a bookkeeper and Marie worked as a telephone operator. The Kellers were a typical middle-class family, living at 2617 E. 122nd St. in Cleveland. Within 5 years the household had already expanded, with the couple having two children in rapid succession, Julia and John, (born in 1913 and 1914 respectively), by the time Theresa arrived.

Tess Keller, Margaret Keller & Tommy Roach (Cousin)
Lake Erie, Ohio – Circa 1920's

On April 6, 1917, the USA entered the Great War ("The War to End All Wars," later of course known as World War I). John Keller dutifully completed and submitted his draft registration card in June, describing himself as tall and stout, with blue eyes and light hair. He claimed exemption from duty, stating he had a wife and three young children dependent on him. Marie was again pregnant when, on October 30, 1917, John, then employed as a salesman with the Cleveland Provision Company, died of massive shock after a building collapsed on him. He was only 26. John was buried at Cleveland's Calvary Cemetery, where his parents (his father would die the following year) would also be interred. John and Marie's fourth child, Margaret was born posthumously the following year, leaving Marie a widow with four small children at the age of 23.

While the details of Theresa's early childhood are somewhat vague, it is known that she attended both public schools and the Villa Angela Academy. Villa Angela was a boarding school and academy for girls, founded in the mid-1870s by the Ursuline Sisters of Cleveland. Originally built on property purchased by the Sisters on the south shore of

Villa Angela Academy

16

Lake Erie, it would remain there until the school moved to a new building in 1972. In 1990, Villa Angela merged with the all-male St. Joseph High School and is presently a private Roman Catholic college preparatory school.

Theresa would later recall frequenting art museums, adding "her parents" considered her and her creative aspirations to be "crack-brained and unstable." As Theresa's father had died when Joan was an infant, it can only be assumed she was referring to her mother and stepfather, whom Marie had married when Theresa was 15, or a careless reporter had embellished his story. Theresa's paternal aunt Florence Keller King later recalled that even as a child Theresa was interested in art, and vividly recalled pictures drawn with great attention by the small child.

In October 1929, Theresa was a month shy of her 13th birthday when the Roaring Twenties came to a screeching halt with the plummet of the stock market. With a sickening thud, that heady era of Fitzgerald and flaming flappers, overnight millionaires, bootleggers and, as Fitzgerald put it, those hedonistic 'Bright Young People with a Talent for Living' who had frenetically danced the Charleston atop cocktail tables when Lindbergh landed in Paris just a few years earlier, vanished overnight. The lights went out on a decade that had briefly defined a nation. In its stead arrived the dark, stark, desperate world that would be known to history as the Great Depression.

Ohio had been hit especially hard by the financial crisis. In 1932, 37% of Ohio's population were jobless. By 1933, over 40% of factory workers and over 67% of construction workers found themselves unemployed, while 50% of industrial workers in Cleveland and 80% in Toledo alone found themselves in the same desperate situation. As a result, many of Ohio's urban residents would leave in search of a more promising environment, desperate to be able to provide food and shelter for their families. Marie, who by then had been a widow for over 14 years, had developed an affectionate, but, according to family members most likely a platonic relationship with a divorced Wisconsin painter, Joseph P. Bernier. Family tradition is that Bernier was chronically ill and probably didn't have long to live. Nevertheless, he and Marie married in Cleveland on April 5, 1932.

Marie Roach Keller & Second Husband
Joseph Bernier

Unsurprisingly, six month later she again found herself a widow when Bernier died on November 28, 1932. Marie buried her second husband, as she had her first, at Calvary Cemetery.

Despite Bernier's death, life in the Keller family apparently moved forward with little change. While it may be assumed Theresa graduated from Villa Angela in or around 1934, there evidently were no spare funds for any higher education. Theresa later recalled she had enjoyed sculpting since she was a child, but it seems likely that she didn't have any professional training until 1934, when she was 17 or 18. If the legend is factual, it came about in a storybook manner.

The regionally well-known sculptress and costume designer Miriam E. Cramer (born in 1885, a native of Germany) had studied at the Cleveland School of Art, as well as in Philadelphia and New York. In the few photographs available, Cramer appears to be a rather intimidating person of a certain age, with hair parted severely down the middle and bushy eyebrows. Her brief encounter with Theresa's began according to later press reports, when, on a whim, Theresa strolled into Cramer's Cleveland studio while Cramer was in the midst of

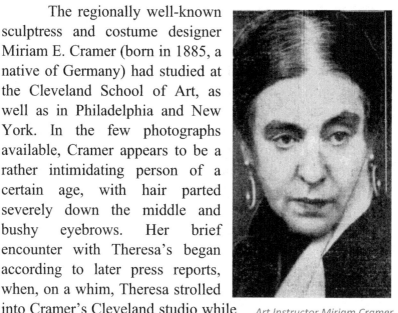

Art Instructor Miriam Cramer

conducting a sculpting class. Taken with Theresa, Cramer apparently offered her a month's free tuition (or possibly an agreement in exchange for some housekeeping chores), which Theresa eagerly accepted. At the end of that month, Theresa's first taste of professional guidance came to an end. While Cramer only instructed her for that very brief time, later news stories would often note Theresa had been a protégée of Cramer.

While Ohio's economy continued to stagnate, Theresa's eldest sister Julia had begun seriously seeing a young man, Cyril Brickman, a friend of her brother John. With opportunities so bleak in Cleveland, Cyril and John decided to head south to Florida (their heads no doubt filled with visions of palm trees and balmy breezes), with the understanding that Julia, her mother, and sisters would soon follow. The young men arrived in Miami in January 1935 and secured work as commercial painters. Marie and her daughters followed in March. The 1935 Florida census shows the Keller family and Cyril living at 6321 NW 23 Ave., north of downtown Miami (the home no longer exists; the present house on the site was built in 1967). Julia and Cyril would marry within a year (in Miami on February 15, 1936), but a more unconventional road laid ahead for Theresa. Around this time, Theresa began using a new first name, choosing to be known as Joan. Theresa likely never

Cyril Brickman & Julia Keller

dreamed that within a few short years, the newly renamed
Joan Keller would find herself the latest Cinderella Girl of
Florida's Art World.

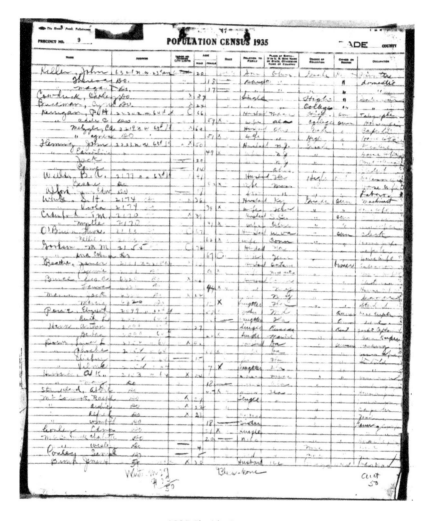

1935 Florida Census

SCULPTRESS FORGOTTEN

CHAPTER 3

SCULPTRESS IN TRAINING, MIAMI, CORAL GABLES, 1935-1938

SCULPTRESS IN TRAINING, MIAMI, CORAL GABLES, 1935-1938

Cyril Brickman and the Keller family did not stay at the NW 23 Avenue house for long, moving soon after the Keller family's arrival to what appears to have been a duplex at 940 NE 83 Street. This house, when photographed in June 2015, appears to be of the same period and style of the time, but public records indicate it was built in 1936. In any event, Cyril, Marie and her four children were living at that address by August 1935.

That August would prove to be a turning point in 18-year-old Joan's future. On a sweltering August 15th, the afternoon edition of the Miami Daily News (the "Daily" was later dropped from the masthead) announced that the judges for the Daily News Arts Contest had been selected. Five men and women had accepted the invitation of the Miami News and the Miami Academy of Arts to serve as judges for the submitted works of aspiring artists who were no older than twenty. An exhibition of the artists' works would be on display at the Academy's building at 328 NE 2 Ave. (the site is presently part of Miami-Dade College's Wolfson campus) and would remain open to the public until August 23rd.

Among the judges was Elizabeth Carolyn "Carrie" Hertenstein Lumley (1887-1964), a prominent art instructor at the Miami Academy of Arts. A native of Davidson Co., TN, she attended public school in Davidson County and studied art at the Watkins Institute (now the Watkins College of Art, Design & Film) in Nashville. According to her obituary, she taught at the Miami Institute of Art. Twice widowed, her second husband, Dean Lumley died in 1943.

24

Not long thereafter she returned to Nashville, where she was an artist for Nashville portrait photographers. From the late 1940s she had suffered from ill health for many years before dying of a heart attack in January 1964.

JOAN KELLER, 18, WINNER IN NEWS ART EXHIBITION

Despite heavy rains, a large crowd braved the weather to attend the final ceremony on August 23rd. The following morning, headlines announced "*JOAN KELLER, 18, WINNER IN NEWS ART EXHIBITION*". Described as a delicate blonde girl, who had only formally studied art for two months during her 18 years, Joan took the top honors with her impressionistic charcoal drawing entitled "Woman at Rest". The grand prize was three lessons a week for six months in art study under Elizabeth Lumley (the second prize was for 4 months study and third prize two months.) It was the first headline of Joan's career.

It may reasonably be assumed that Joan took advantage of her prize and studied with Lumley for six months. If so, it would then have been in 1936 that she became a student at the Miami Federal Galleries. Located at 100 NE 1st Avenue, the Federal Galleries was the first major Federal building to be constructed in Miami. Completed in 1914, the neo-classical building was widely considered to be the most modern government building in the South. When it opened, the

Elizabeth C. Lumely

U.S. Post Office occupied the first floor, the Federal Court the second, while other government offices occupied the third floor. In 1931 the Federal Government relocated to larger premises two blocks away. From 1931 to 1937, when the building was sold to First Federal Savings & Loan (which eventually became AmeriFirst Federal), it was occupied by various government offices. The former second-floor District Courtroom was leased for $1 a year by "old-age pension" organizations for use as a cultural center, including a library and art exhibition space. On March 31, 1936, it was announced that the City Commission had authorized the City Manager to negotiate new quarters for these "old-age pension" organizations, so that this second-floor could be turned over to the WPA for use as an art gallery. The building would become an important venue for many aspiring artists, including Joan.

It is interesting to digress a moment to recount the subsequent history of this landmark building. After being sold in 1937 to First Federal, the building served in a variety of capacities, including as a branch of the future AmeriFirst and as an Office Depot, but was often underused or empty. In 2000, Miami native and South Beach developer Scott Robins purchased the neglected, nearly 90-year-old building for $1,650,000. Founder of the Scott Robins Companies, he considered himself a preservationist and a leader in "transforming blighted and forgotten areas into newly important metropolitan centers."

Miami Federal Galleries; Formerly the U.S. Post Office and Courthouse

In 2012 Robins negotiated a five-year lease for the first two floors with the Miami Chapter of the American Institute of Architects (AIA). The non-profit AIA spent over $300,000 renovating the two floors an opened the Miami Center for Architecture (MCAD). In the process, contractors ripped off vinyl flooring, discovering pristine white marble floors, removed unsightly drop ceilings to reveal the original majestic arches and 16-foot ceilings, and then added some complementary contemporary touches of their own.

MCAD held their first exhibition there in December 2013. Only six months later Robins sold the building to Stambul Ventures LLC for an impressive $11,000,000, ten times what he had paid for it. Three years later, when the AIA's lease came up for renewal in December 2017, Stambul, in a surprising and controversial move, declined to renew it. Corporate filings stated Stambul's agent was Daniel Pena, named as Stambul's manager, with an address on Brickell Avenue. The AIA was livid, while Stambul representatives could not be reached for comment. In May 2018 press reports announced that Stambul had inked a five-year lease agreement, with two five-year tenant renewal options with Biscayne Bay Brewery, based in Doral, to open a brewery and bar on the third floor. The AIA was unceremoniously ousted from the 116-year-old building they had done much to restore, or as the Miami Herald succinctly stated, were left "crying in their beer."

Rewinding the clock to 1936, the Miami Federal Galleries (also initially referred to as the WPA Art Gallery), held their official opening on April 26th. Those in attendance were pleasantly surprised at the quality of the paintings on display. From 150 pieces submitted for consideration, the four-judge panel selected 67 works by artists from across Florida. The work was sufficiently fine to convince attendees that the new Gallery was a promising development in the direction of *"a side of Miami's life yet all too much neglected."*

In covering the event, the Miami News informed the public that in addition to the gallery space, WPA would conduct instructional art classes were three evenings a week, at a cost of 10 cents per student (exclusive of paper and charcoal). Attendance grew from 29 to 57 students in the first week. These classes would provide those unable to afford private instruction with the opportunity to discover and develop their innate talent. In turn, it was reasoned, the private studios' classes would benefit by stimulating interest in the arts in general. The article concluded, *"These enterprises deserve encouragement if Miami is to become as well known for its cultural advantages as for its dog tracks and slot machines."*

As the Galleries were sponsored by the WPA, many of the instructors volunteered their time and talent. Among those instructors was one whose name would be intertwined with Coral Gables for more than 50 years – Richard Merrick (1903-1986), youngest brother of the City's father, George Merrick. Richard was emerging as a renowned oil painter

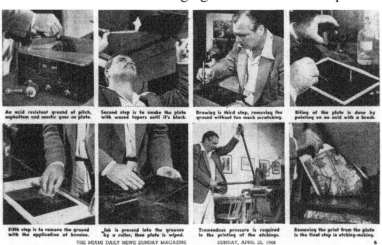

Richard Merrick Demonstrating His Artistic Abilities

29

and was associated with the Federal Gallery as early as May 1936, when he spoke to large audience on modern painting.

On June 21, 1936, The WPA held a special "Mayors' Night" reception at the Galleries, with an exhibition showcasing the accomplishments of the WPA's Fourth District, which encompassed Dade, Broward, and Collier counties. Officials from the District, members of the Women's City Club of Greater Miami, and other dignitaries greeted guests in what must have been a lengthy receiving line. Included were Mayors A.D. Fosse of Miami and Robert Brunstetter of Coral Gables, as well as the mayors of Miami Beach, North Miami, Miami Springs, Miami Shores, Fort Lauderdale, and Hollywood. Among the others receiving the Galleries' guests were Joan, prominent architect Phineas Paist (1873-1937, who worked extensively with George Merrick in Coral Gables) and Eve Alsman Fuller (1898-1947, well-known art critic, newspaper editor and the State Director of the Federal Art Project.) The ten-day exhibit on the second floor was visited with great enthusiasm by over 700 people each evening.

Eve Alsman Fuller; Florida State Director of the Federal Art Project

The artists at the Galleries were busy that summer. In June, mural decorations for the "receiving home" of the Southeastern Branch of the Florida Children's Home Society were discussed at a meeting held by the Woman's Club of Greater Miami, who agreed to sponsor the project. The home was overseen by the Junior League and located at NW 14th Street and 8th

Avenue. The Society assisted in providing housing, seeking out foster parents and striving to assure that the needs of these underserved children were addressed. It was agreed that Rosebud Clephane (1898-1972), Chair of the Galleries' life class would supervise the project. The Galleries' Director, the debonair, pencil-thin mustached Francois de Brouliette, would oversee general supervision of the project.

"Young Miami Artists Are Painting Murals of Nursery Rhymes To Decorate Walls of Children's Home Here" was the headline for a lengthy featured human-interest story by reporter Betty Tufts Bouchard in the Miami Herald's Sunday paper on September 6, 1936. The opening paragraph set the tone for the article. *"Everyone 'loves a parade' but when that one is a youngster living in a Children's Home and, perhaps, too ill to play, the parade must come marching and dancing across nursery walls so that little hearts may grow light and childish eyes may sparkle with glee."*

The reporter informed readers those were the thoughts of a group of young artists from the Miami Federal Galleries. The Woman's Club of Greater Miami pitched in by supplying paint, brushes and canvases. Clephane invited every member of the Life Classes to submit designs, and reported *"the response was thrilling,"* and several were selected as the most suitable for the spaces. Actual work had begun several weeks earlier in the Galleries' annex. As it was not practical to execute the actual painting directly on the walls of the home, those artists who were donating their time and talent would complete their murals on wall board, which would be installed in the home when completed.

Bouchard continued, *"Only young artists – not too many years removed from the joyous playdays of childhood – could create such gay, delightful conceptions. Almost one hears the rat-tat-tat of the drums and the shrill laughter of the merry clowns. Baby hands will reach for the bright nodding balloons. There are* prancing *ponies, tigers in cages – all in bright clear color against an azure background."*

There were five designers who were responsible for creating the panels to be painted. "The Circus Parade" was created by William Schael (1914-2001), Rosebud Clephane composed a "Santa Claus" theme set of panels, "The Five Little Pigs" by Mildred Prindle, a "Mother Goose" theme panel was the work of Dulcie Bandel (1919-2002) and "Alice in Wonderland" was envisioned by Evelyn Andreas (c.1908-1951). Once these sizable boards were completed, a team of the galleries' artists went work with the actual painting. Once installed, the murals would decorate four rooms of the home.

Those who did the actual painting on these panels were Evelyn Andreas, Allen M. Beattie, Rosebud Clephane, Joy Pellot, Jean Hall, Joseph Hoy, Kathleen Tremblay, and Joan. As Bouchard noted, *"These young people are donating several hours of their time daily in the carrying forward of this work."* Noted muralist and marine and landscape painter Chester J. Tingler of Miami Beach (1886-1966) served as chief onsite advisor to the group. By the time this featured article appeared, several of the large panels were practically completed, while others had just begun. Interested visitors were welcome to see the works in progress on the second floor of the Galleries, where the artists would be found busily at work every day.

In addition to their work, the Miami Federal Galleries garnered a good bit of positive notice in the summer of 1936. Particularly interesting was an article in the Miami Herald of June 28th. Reporter Henry Cavendish wrote that, in a quiet manner, devoid of ballyhoo and blustering, an art movement which had no counterpart outside of New York, Chicago and a few other metropolitan areas in the country, was developing in Miami. He predicted this new movement was likely to revolutionize the activities which fell under the Federal Art Program of the WPA. These were not faddish artistes, noted Cavendish, who reported *"Nor are its devotees the long-fingered figures with flowing hair and flaring bow ties such as are ordinarily associated with artistic movements emanating from the Parisian Latin Quarter of gilded and glamorous fame.*

Rather, the Miami movement is centered in a large cavernous hall on the second floor of the old post office building annex – right in the center of the downtown business district. And its adherents are ordinary, everyday Miamians having an interest in art, who go about their accustomed affairs throughout the days of the week and gather on Mondays, Wednesdays and Friday nights to pursue studies in line and form, in color and in the various media of artistic expression."

Under the direction of the Galleries' director, Francois de Brouliette, the original proponent of establishing the art center, and who created the curriculum, enrollment in the art classes had exceeded 700 students, ranging from children to adults. There were classes in mask-making, lettering, sculpturing, marionettes and even fencing. The life classes, held three times a week, were by far the most popular, with early enrollments exceeding 250 aspiring students. Two instructors were on hand for guidance and assistance. In addition to de Brouliette, they included Chester Tingler, Eric Burtis, Richard Merrick and several others, including Amadeo Reyes, whose specialty was working with Spanish-speaking students in their native tongue – demonstrating that over two decades before the influx of Cuban nationals fleeing to safety in the wake of Castro seizing power at the dawn of 1959, Miami already had a taste of being bi-lingual.

Without question, Joan's passion was the life-classes, a preference which would be true for the rest of her career. As such, it is worthwhile quoting Henry Cavendish's article about these sessions at some length. "...*the students work directly from life, employing a model for the two hours' work of the triweekly sessions. Each of the students contributes 10 cents to pay the model, and in this way they are enabled to do their sketches and paintings directly from life instead of working from copies. There is a small charge, running usually around 5 or 10 cents for each session, for drawing paper and other necessary materials. The instruction, however, is furnished free along with the art center quarters in the gallery annex, which provides an opportunity for the students collectively to employ a model at comparatively little cost to the individuals. "The scene in the gallery annex on the occasion of one of the life classes is one familiar in the art schools of Chicago and New York, Paris and Rome. Yet is a scene rarely encountered in the smaller cities and towns scattered over the map of the United States.*

"*In their role as the actors in this scene, members of the Federal Arts project's life class go unperturbed, almost stolidly about their business, sketching in lines and angles on the drawing paper pinned to drawing boards propped up before them. The shape of an arm, the curve of a hip in limned in almost with business-like disinterestedness. Lines are erased, and other lines truer to form are sketched in their stead. Perspective is gauged, and the various phases on the art problem under consideration are studied exhaustively.*

"*Almost in the center of the annex hall is a raised platform on which the model stands, sits or reclines. A masculine model is studied one night, a feminine model another night. Overhead the glaring rays of two dazzling white arc lights shine down upon the model, revealing every line and curve and angle in vivid outline. The lift of a muscle casts back its shadow, the turn of a shoulder throws a shade below.*

"*It's somewhat like that – the model there on the raised platform, still as a statue, immobile as though frozen in there under the relentless revelation of the glaring arc lights. The lights however, are shaded so that but little of the glare reaches the eyes of the working students. The students themselves as gathered astride of little benches, making a complete ring around the model and the platform. Their drawing boards are propped up at an angle leaning away from them, the degree of the angle adjusted to suit the desires of the particular student.*

"*Commencing promptly at 7:30 p.m., the model takes the position on the raised platform, and the students begin their evening work. For 20 minutes, the model, once having assumed the directed pose, remains as still as a statue while the students work away. There follows a rest period of 10 minutes, wherein the model is allowed to relax and rest. The rest period ended, the pose is resume [sic] and again the students work fast in an effort to catch every detail and outline of the pose before it is changed. Occasionally, they pause to survey the results of their sketching, but the pauses are brief."*

While the students were working, visitors wandered about the gallery and its annex, looking at the art on display, peering over the artists' shoulders, and during the ten-minute breaks for the model every twenty minutes, often engaging the students in conversation. Although not identified by name, Cavendish's description of one of the students sounds tantalizingly like Joan.

Cavendish concluded his lengthy article with *"And so the picture of the present fades into the mystic shadows of the night-time, perhaps to give way to a greater vision of the future wherein the studies sponsored by the Miami Federal Galleries will prove but the nucleus of the establishment here of a new of culture and of artistic learning."*

Important Administrative changes to the Miami Federal Galleries were announced at the end of August 1936. William Wood, Supervisor of the Federal Art Project District 3 (which encompassed, Dade, Broward, Palm Beach and Monroe counties, informed the public that Francois de Brouillette, the Galleries' founding director, was being replaced by Adam Empie (1876-1943), the former publicity officer of the Galleries. The news came as a surprise to many. At the same time, State Director Eve Alsman Fuller also announced that Chester Tingler would head the new mural project division and that Lampert Bemelmans (of whom more shortly) would take over as Project Supervisor for Sculpting. While no confirming records have been located, it is likely that, when Bemelmans' appointment took effect, Joan joined his staff in the Sculpture Division.

CORAL GABLES WOMAN'S CLUB PLAQUE

Eric Burtis Presenting a Bronze Plaque to the Coral Gables Women's Club; June 1936.

In the wake of these changes, the following month it was announced that the WPA art classes would resume offering free classes to eligible students, with 50-year-old California born sculptor Eric Forsyth Burtis (1884-1960) instructing in sculpting. While it cannot be definitively proven Joan was student of Burtis, they did know each other well through the late 1930s and early 1940s.

Burtis, who had edited and published the first textbooks on naval aviation while he was an ensign during

WWI, would garner some interesting press during World War II, when, in 1942, he designed "smother bombs," comprised of sand encased in plaster of Paris, designed to fight the deadly magnesium incendiary bombs. Each of these bombs were filled with over 5 pounds of sand to combat the flames from the incendiary bombs. Despite his forays into military affairs, Burtis is best remembered for his artwork, particularly a 1956 sculptured bas-relief of President Dwight Eisenhower.

It was during 1936, while still in her formative years, that Joan revealed her obsessive strive for perfection, and in the adage that 'experience teaches.' Moving further away from painting and concentrating of sculpting, Keller would experiment in solitude on hewing from rock until she was completely satisfied with the finished work. However, she was rarely completely contented. Her aunt, Florence King, would recall rescuing a self-portrait in plaster of Paris when the young artist tried to destroy it due to a perceived lack of perfection. People who knew her years later would say Keller hardly appeared to age as she grew older, looking almost the same as she did in this early self-portrait.

On October 8th, the officers and members of the Art Students League of Miami held a reception at the Galleries, to tie in with the exhibition then showcasing a representative body of work from both the New York and the Miami art students' leagues. With the cooperation of State Director Eve Fuller, guests had the opportunity of comparing selected oils and prints by the Miami league with those of their New York counterparts. Among the nine or so Miami artists were Joan, and Kenneth DeGarmo (1913-1991), 23-year-old son of famed architect Walter DeGarmo (1876-1951). Over a decade earlier, Walter had been one of George Merrick's most prominent architects, designing some of the most sought-after residences in Coral Gables during the Merrick era. Together with Merrick's uncle, George Denman Fink (1880-1956), the senior DeGarmo had also designed the imposing Douglas Entrance to Coral Gables.

When the Miami Federal Galleries lost their space at the former Post Office in early 1937 after the building's sale to First Federal, Director Adam Empie stated to the press on May 15 that due to this loss of their facilities, the Galleries were at a critical crossroads. Empie stated bluntly the future of the project, which had groomed many talented artists, including Joan, would be dependent on the support and interest Miami residents evidenced in their various cultural and educational activities.

The ousted students were surely sympathetic to the Galleries' plight. However, it must be remembered they were, for the most part, determined, strong-minded and while young, had been toughened by enduring and surviving the Great Depression. That July several of the students who had worked at the Galleries joined forces and formed The Studio Guild, housed above Jack's Garage, 19 SW 2nd Street. Under the headline "*Miami Studio Guild Bans Bohemian Atmosphere for the More Serious Pursuit and Study of Art*", the location was described in contemporary accounts as a "*big, bare loft above a storage garage. There are white-washed rafters and a rough board floor, and the corners beyond the reach of the floodlights illuminating the model stand are dim, and, quite possibly, hung with cobwebs. It is all extremely atmospheric and Greenwich Village – in appearance, but the romantic art effect stops right there. It*

*is an extremely earnest co-operative effort on the part of
sincere students of art. Neither school nor club, it partakes
a little of the nature of both.*

"*There is only one requirement for membership,*" the
September 4th article continued, "but that one is sternly
enforced. Those who enter the door beneath the sign of the
paint daubed palette and climb the twisty stairs, must be
seriously interested in art. Nothing is said about previous
experience or amount of talent. Experience can be had at the
guild, and talent is between the artist and his Maker, but there
must be no question of the strength of purpose of a guild
member. No dabblers, hobbyists or new sensation seekers
are welcome."

The most recent addition to Miami's growing art
movement, The Studio Guild was composed of these
enthusiastic young artists who decided to step up and form
their own organization, which was entirely cooperative and
existed only for their mutual benefit in art study. The Life
Classes, which were seemingly modeled after those at the
Galleries, met every Monday, Wednesday, and Friday
evenings, while watercolor and oil classes met in the
afternoons. A nominal fee of a few cents paid for the model.
While there could be as many as 50 students at the life class
sessions (using curious contraptions that served as both seat
and easel), triflers and dilettantes were definitely not only
unwelcome, but actively discouraged from participating.

Two art instructors who had taught under the WPA
guided the work of the group – Chester Tingler and Richard
Merrick. At the same time, Merrick was in charge of the
teaching schedule for the Miami Federal Galleries in Coral
Gables, housed at the University of Miami, which Richard's

brother George had founded 11 years earlier. Until 1949, the main campus of the University was located on and around University Drive, with some buildings (notably the San Sebastian Apartments) on or near LeJeune Road.

The same article specifically homed in on Joan. *"Over in the corner Joan Keller, the young sculptor in blue pants and shirt, is crouched on a stool, delicately pecking away with a chisel and mallet. Her taffy-candy colored hair bobs rhythmically with every stroke and several of her colleagues hover anxiously over her. Obviously, something crucial is taking place."*

The Studio Guild had no budget, its officers served without compensation and six of them personally guaranteed the rent and other costs would be paid. Most of the members were employed in some capacity, most in occupations, directly or otherwise connected with the arts, and spent every possible moment at the Guild studio. Many held on to their day jobs at a significant sacrifice because they did not want to lose touch with their art. They needed the sustaining sense that the importance of art was being felt in the community. All they wanted was encouragement and recognition of *"their right and place in the south Florida sun"*. For a few of them, including Joan, that was precisely what happened, resulting in major recognition for a year or longer. For most of the aspirants however, their 15 minutes of fame came and went far too quickly.

Of more immediate impact to Joan's career was Lambert Bemelmans (1871-1951), a noted Miami sculptor and painter, who in August 1936 had been named as Supervisor of Sculpturing for the Federal Arts Project, which, together with the Miami Federal Galleries, worked under the auspices of the WPA. Bemelmans (also spelled in some contemporaneous accounts as Bemmelman), a native of Belgium, had a rather checkered past. According to accounts by his son, Ludwig (Louis) Bemelmans (1898-1962), who would become famous as the author of the popular 'Madeline' book series, Lambert impregnated both his wife (Ludwig's mother) and the family governess, then deserted both for another woman. The governess, whom Ludwig adored, committed suicide. In December 1904, Lambert and his second wife Emma (Emmy) emigrated from Belgium to the United States, settling in New York. In 1916, he petitioned the United States for Naturalization. He stated he and his wife lived on W. 182nd Street, and that he had two sons – Ludwig, who was then 18 and living with his father and stepmother, and Oskar (b. 1903), who was born just a year before Lampert emigrated. Oskar was living in Germany, which raises the question if his mother was perhaps the third woman in Lampert's life.

Bemelmans moved to Miami in 1925, the frenzied height of the Florida Land Boom. Over the next ten years he created several memorable pieces of art, including several plaques at Jackson Memorial Hospital, the Earhart plaque at Amelia Earhart Field in Hialeah, the Carl Fisher plaque at Miami Beach City Hall, and the fountain at the Coral Gables Woman's Club. Among his most recent work for 1936 was the Keys Memorial Monument.

While Bemelmans' reputation as a respected sculptor was impeccable, his behavior in his private life would greatly affect his son Ludwig. Decades later when his 'Madeline' books were quite popular, Ludwig would write to Jacqueline Kennedy, "For me, Madeline is therapy in the dark hours".

Despite his marital and extra-marital issues, Lambert's career as a sculptor flourished during the Depression, with some of his most notable work being done in Coral Gables and The Florida Keys. More importantly to this story, from 1936 through 1939 Lampert, well into his 60s and still married to Emma, was frequently noted in the press as the mentor and frequent companion of Joan, a talented young woman just entering her twenties and on the cusp of widespread recognition.

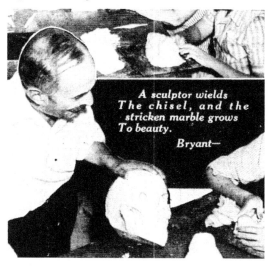

A sculptor wields The chisel, and the stricken marble grows To beauty.

Bryant—

Sculptor Ludwig Bemelmans, Florida Art Project WPA

SCULPTRESS FORGOTTEN

CHAPTER 4

FAME BECKONS, CORAL GABLES, 1938-1939

SCULPTRESS FORGOTTEN

FAME BECKONS, CORAL GABLES, 1938-1939

As noted earlier, In November 1937, the WPA received an application and conditionally approved funding for a proposed new police station for Coral Gables, to be located on the northeast corner of Aragon and Salzedo. Work began the beginning of March 1938. The total cost was estimated at $42,958, of which the federal allowance was $30,787 and the sponsor's portion $12,170. Native keystone, which had been greatly depleted in Coral Gables, was hauled up from Windley Key. The stone came from the same quarry as that used for Lampert Bemelman's Keys Memorial Monument on Matecumbee Key, which had been unveiled the previous November to honor over 500 victims (many of whom were veterans sent to work in the Keys by the WPA) of the 1935 hurricane. Of those who perished, the cremated remains of 190 were interred at the Memorial site.

A month later Coral Gables gifted the existing police station, located at 2102 Salzedo, to the WPA, who announced it would be renovated by them at a cost of $24,000 and repurposed to become the new home of the Miami Federal Galleries. After the sale of the original Miami Post Office in 1937, the Galleries had been given temporary refuge at the Miami Women's Club on Bayshore Drive. The refurbished building was also to be known as the Art Center of Coral Gables. The Coral Gables Chamber of Commerce spearheaded a steering committee to move this forward to completion. This building has sometimes been misidentified with a still existing building at 303 Alhambra Circle, now much altered, which is presently home to the American Legion Post 98. This is an incorrect assumption, as the American Legion has occupied the structure since 1928. It did, however, serve as the first City Hall, from 1925 until the present City Hall was completed in 1928. It subsequently became the Police and Fire Station from 1928 until they took possession of the completed new structure in March 1939, In April, just a month after the opening of the new Municipal Building, a sculpture and ceramic group was housed in the former station, while a satellite office at 330 Alhambra Circle had a group of eight employees creating an index of American design (the existing building on this site dates from 1956.)

Original Coral Gables City Hall, 1923-1928. In 1928, it became the Police and Fire Station until the Municipal Building was created in 1939.

As for the new Municipal Building, the WPA and President Roosevelt approved the completion of the new building, per a telegram received on June 6, 1938 from Florida's U.S. Senator Claude Pepper. The WPA regional director stated the new complex would be completed before the end of the year. Federal contribution was estimated to be $69,990, and that of Coral Gables $19,551; figures that

are significantly different from the initial approval by the
WPA in November 1937. The reason most likely had to do
with the fact that the new building was initially supposed to
simply replace the existing police department. By June
1938, the scope of the project had enlarged. The Herald
reported "*$80,450 GIVEN FOR FIRE HOUSE – Coral
Gables Project is Approved By WPA; Will Employ 110.*"
The Associated Press broke the news on June 30th. It noted
that the police station was already nearing completion, and
that work would start shortly on the adjoining two-story
fire station. The WPA was supplying $60,990 (or $69,990 –
both numbers have been published) and would employ 110
men for eight months. However, contemplation of
combining the two departments into one complex must
have been in the works much earlier. The earliest
renderings by Phineas Paist, who died in the spring of
1937, clearly show the building appearing almost identical
to the finished project.

The architectural team of Paist & Steward had drawn
up designs for the complex, a blend of Depression-Moderne
and Mediterranean Revival styles, well before the final WPA
approval for the new fire station. Phineas Paist, who was said
to be the first registered architect in Miami, was the primary
designer for the building. A survivor of the Merrick era, he
was well known for his work on, among many other
buildings, Vizcaya (as an associate architect), Douglas
Entrance, the Venetian Pool, and the impressive new City
Hall. Between 1924 and 1937, Paist and his younger partner
Harold Steward were also responsible for the Coral Gables
Woman's Club, the 1931 U.S. Courthouse, Tropical Park,
and many other notable structures. Sadly, Paist would not
live to see the Municipal Building, one of the last of his

masterworks completed. He died on May 2, 1937 aged 64 and was buried in Pennsylvania. it would be left to Harold Steward to oversee the building's completion.

Phineas Paist   *Harold Steward*

One piece of the exterior's design certainly survived from the original concept. On the second floor of the exterior Salzedo side of the building, Paist had always envisioned oversized sculptural keystone reliefs of two fireman, dominating other, smaller reliefs representing the families they served, together with a few more whimsical works. Joan did other reliefs and carvings across the entire exterior, including a bas-relief of pelicans over the main entrance and is the only known sculptor credited as working on the building.

It has virtually become an urban myth that Joan Keller applied for the job of sculpting the "Firemen" sculptures under the name John Keller (the given name of her brother and her late father), perhaps thinking her chances were better at landing the commission if it was assumed the artist was male. While possible, Joan was already a very well-known artist and it is questionable if such subterfuge would have been necessary. Certainly, it was as Joan Keller that she was recognized as the artist. The genesis of the story may generate from the fact that in later years she did indeed use the name Jon Keller and Jon Keller Louie, but her use of these alternative names only came several years later. The suggestion that she used the name Jon Keller in relationship was definitively put to rest in March 2018 when a close inspection of both busts show they were simply chiseled "Joan", followed by the Roman numerals for 1938.

Whether it was through the suggestion or intercession of such influential friends such as Richard Merrick, Eric Burtis, Phineas Paist, Harold Steward or Lambert Bemelman, or if it was simply that the powers that be recognized her already noted talent, there was no question that when her "Firemen" were unveiled, the status of Joan's career would go from widespread, but primarily local, popularity to that of regional, if not national, attention. This work could mean that, for Joan at least, the Great Depression would be ending early. She was only 22 years old.

President Roosevelt approved a $30,878 contribution grant, for the new Gables Municipal Building on January 29, 1938. Initial reports said the new building would house only a new police facility, with the fire department remaining at the Alcazar address. However, by the time actual construction of the new Municipal Building began the week of March 20, 1938, using quarry keystone (also known as coral limestone or coral rock), the fire department facilities had been unofficially added, as originally envisioned by

Paist, to the new building. The two-story main building's ground floor would provide three bays for fire trucks, hook & ladder equipment, a fire prevention room, the fire chief's office, a fire alarm room, mess hall, kitchen, and detention room. Rising from the Fire Department (the Salzedo side) would be a 50-foot Tower. The Coral Gable Police Department also had offices on the ground floor, accessed by a lobby with a large booking desk, an office for the chief of police, an auto inspection department, lockers and bathroom facilities, a police station, a courtroom with an antechamber, an identification bureau, a bull pen (the large cell where prisoners were detained while waiting to be brought into the court room), four cell blocks (segregated by race and sex), and shops. The press noted that all the furnishings and equipment would be modern, creating new efficiency for both departments.

While Joan was waiting to begin sculpting her "Firemen", she kept busy. In early April she was in Palm Beach attending an exhibition staged by the Society of Four Arts, hosted in tandem with the Palm Beach Art League. Focused on works by Florida artists, the exhibition ran from April 3rd through the 17th. Joan was prominently noted for her marble sculpture entitled "Forever Dead," with the piece being called "part of a number of outstandingly fine pieces of sculpture."

On the world front, storm clouds were brewing when, on March 13th, Hitler annexed Austria, but stateside a Depression weary people, remembering the Great War only 20 years earlier and, avidly represented by a strong Isolationist party, chose to let Europe deal as they would with an aggressive Germany. Closer to home, on April 30th, Joan's youngest sister Margaret married Raymond (Ray, a.k.a. Russell) Charles Washburn, a Hartford, CT. native seven years her senior, on April 30th at the Courthouse in Everglades, FL, then the county seat of Collier County. It was a quiet ceremony, with the presiding official's wife serving as a witness, and it is doubtful Joan, her mother or siblings attended.

Tess Keller, Ray Washburn, Julia Keller Brickman, Mrs. Washburn
(Ray's mother). Miami, FL – Circa 1940s

Back in Coral Gables, work was proceeding rapidly on the Police & Fire Station. On July 15, 1938, with a sizeable crowd in attendance, a cornerstone laying ceremony was held, presided over by Mayor Paul McGarry while a Federal Theater orchestra provided entertainment. Members of the police and fire departments lined up at attention on Aragon, while a pump engine from the fire department was drawn up at the Salzedo curb. According to the Miami Herald, Coral Gables was contributing $31,721 and the Federal Government $91,777. In his remarks, Mayor McGarry, referring to both a recent bond settlement and the new building, stated "With all these developments coming along together, it looks as though the bright future of Coral Gables was [sic] assured."

While Joan Is not mentioned as attending (the eastern wall of the building that would display "The Firemen" had not yet been erected), the cornerstone, as far as is known, has remained unopened to the present day. It is said to encase a time capsule, inside of which was a roster of the police, the

Cornerstone Laying Ceremony at the New Municipal Building, July 16, 1938

fire department and city officials, WPA payroll records, drawn detailed plans of the building and a copy of that day's issue of "The Rivera," the local Coral Gables newspaper.

Joan's name was being seen in the press more frequently. She had remained a member of The Studio Guild, the student-controlled, non-profit cooperative art center, that had been founded by former students of the Miami Federal Galleries. At the end of July, she was mentioned as being a member of the Guild's committee for their second annual Beaux Arts Ball and Art Exhibit, with the exhibition starting on September 1st and culminating with a ball at the Royal Palm Club on the 7th. Eve Alsman Fuller, State Director of the Federal Art Project, arrived in Miami on August 16 to confer with sponsors, promising full cooperation and stating the exhibit would create great interest statewide. "*It is a noteworthy achievement in the advance of art between the United States and Latin -American countries*," she told the press and guild members. Already over 40 artists from Cuba alone had accepted invitations to exhibit their art. On September 1st, the much-hyped exhibit opened in the Green Room of the Royal Palm Club to tremendous acclaim. Among the 185 pieces of paintings and sculpture in various mediums on display was Joan's sculpture of a life-size male bust crafted from concrete entitled "Study."

After the weeklong exhibition, the much-anticipated Beaux Arts Ball took place on the evening of the September 7th in the ballroom of the recently renovated Royal Palm Club, located at Biscayne Bay and SE 2nd Street. The main dining room was awash in shimmering turquoise, blue, silver and crimson, while the ballroom was an impressive 110 x 82 feet, complete with stage and double orchestra stands. With

Bayfront Park, Bandshell and Royal Palm Club and Docks, Miami, Florida

The Posh Royal Palm Club 1938

a dining mezzanine, a bar and chic lounge opening onto a marine terrace that followed the shore of Biscayne Bay, it was easy to forget, if only for a short time, that the country was still not free from the greatest economic crisis ever known. Another cloud was now looming in the horizon – the growing menace of Nazi Germany's aggression, not only with Germany, but in all of Europe as well. Despite the Nazi annexation of Austria in March 1938, isolationists were successfully holding their ground and keeping America neutral.

For this evening however, the Depression and the looming shadows of possible war were put aside. The moon was still shining over Miami when over 600 of the most prominent members of Florida's art world, some in colorful costume, others in more traditional black-tie descended upon the Royal Palm Club. They were greeted by scenes replicating the lively, if edgy, cafes of Paris' famous Latin Quarter, and with club attendants attired as fiery Apache dancers. The orchestra members were clothed in pink smocks and black berets. Studio guild members and officers, as well as committee members also wore typical artists' apparel. A grand parade of these costumed guests opened the ball, while a bevy of entertainers represented the ball's theme of "Wine, Women and Song."

The Green Room was packed with admirers who showered the artwork with rave reviews, while the judges assembled to announce the winners. The distinguished panel included Alexander Orr, Jr. (1880-1958, who would briefly serve as Mayor of Miami, stepping in upon Mayor E.G. Sewell's death in office in April 1940 and serving until January 1 1941) Orr was joined by Denman DeLong Fink (1880-1952), George Merrick's uncle and closest collaborator, a nationally renowned artist and illustrator who, over a decade earlier had been a key factor in making his nephew's dream of making Coral Gables a Mediterranean fantasy of grand entrances, plazas and richly themed buildings, into reality. The panel also included internationally renowned landscape artist Ernest Lawson (1872-1939), a Canadian American post-impressionist who had moved to Coral Gables in 1936. Three years later, aged 66, said to be depressed and in declining health, Lawson would drown under mysterious circumstances while swimming along Miami Beach. Close friends considered it probable Lawson had committed suicide.

Eminent and revered judges all, but Fink and Lawson had already had their share of artistic fame that night when the Studio Guild's First Prize for Sculpture was awarded to 21-year-old Joan Keller for "Study". While works from professional artists such as Fink, Lawson, Richard Merrick, and Elizabeth Lumley were included in the exhibit, it was photos of the glowing, beautiful blonde Joan on the threshold of an incredible career which made the newspapers the following morning. The article also noted in passing that Joan lived at 231 NW 24 Avenue (the house, built in 1925 is still standing), whether with members of her family, alone, or with someone else altogether is unknown.

While the exact dates during which Joan created what would become her signature "Firemen" is not known, they logically would have been sculpted sometime in the latter half of 1938. A tantalizing photo appears in long shot in the Miami Herald of someone, presumably Joan, on a scaffold, perhaps positioning or finishing some final details once the busts were in-situ. The sculptures, which were affixed to the exterior wall with rebar, are generally agreed to be the building's most distinctive feature - a prime example of Depression Moderne - somber, direct and realistic, but not without decorative character. Below the busts, at the bases flanking the entrance bays for the firetrucks to enter and exit are, according to lore, stylized metal representations of their empty boots. More practically, these 'boots', if that indeed was their objective, they also served to protect the coral rock exterior from damage by vehicles. Similar 'boots' can still be found throughout Coral Gables.

The "Fireman" busts are said to have been modeled from two actual Coral Gables firemen, one of whose surnames was possibly Kelly. There is no question that the

images of the two Firemen are based two different people. One, arguably the more striking of the pair, has one button of his uniform jacket undone, and has distinctly more chiseled features, especially with his chin, while the one just to north on the facade has his jacket fully buttoned and an obviously softer countenance. The small sculptures surrounding the Firemen, designed to portray a typical family whose lives the Firemen protected, has a subtler subtext. While some of the sculpted heads appear to be simply whimsical (such as a harlequin, the precursor of a clown, said to a trickster who liked to keep everyone they meet off-balance and confused), others seem to be drawn from Joan's own life. These include Joan herself, several animals, including a dog, a cat and a parrot (Joan was later known to be obsessed with all animals, especially cats) and a young man, possibly her brother John.

The five pelicans situated over the main entrance to the building are a clear reference to the lore that Pelicans will deliberately injure themselves with their beaks to draw blood to feed their young – a clear analogy to the police and firemen who put their own lives at risk to protect the public they served.

In October 1938, with Joan's work at the Municipal Building probably near completion, Florida Governor Fred Cone appointed Myrtle Taylor Bradford (1875-1958) as Director of Miami's role in national observance of American Art Week, sponsored by the American Artists Professional League, to be held the week of November 1st through 7th. The purpose of the league was to give young artists the opportunity of displaying their works to the public, and Bradford encouraged Miami Clubs, schools and other venues to participate in showcasing the young artists' artworks. The goal was national enlightenment, to bring governmental and civic recognition to arts and to emphasize by exhibitions the worth of local crafts and fine art. Bradford would shortly become the State Art Director of the American Artists Professional League, serving in that capacity for 18 years.

Bradford and her team would seek the cooperation of merchants, who would be asked to arrange exhibits. Various committees were appointed. Joan, no longer a student or fledgling artist, and Lampert Bemelmans were among those appointed to serve on the Sculpture Committee. Elizabeth Lumley was on the art schools committee. Representing the University of Miami and Coral Gables were Richard Merrick, Chester Tingler and Denman Fink, with Fink also agreeing to be a keynote speaker throughout the week. It was a veritable line-up of the most prominent talent in the Miami area. The exhibit was held at the Miami Federal Galleries, still housed in the Miami Woman's Club at 1737 North Bayshore, while the studio housing the committee for the State Index of American Design, at 303 Alhambra Circle, was also opening their doors to the public for the duration of the exhibit. By the end of its scheduled run, by popular demand the exhibit was extended through November 12th.

By the beginning of January 1939, it appears that any hard feelings that might have been created when former students, including Joan, broke away from the Miami Federal Galleries when they had lost their permanent home July 1937 years earlier had subsided. During the first week of the year, the Federal Galleries hosted a gala at their temporary housing in the Miami Woman's Club. The gala featured a one-man exhibit of watercolor sketches done in China and South America by Jan Porel (1894-1965). A sizeable crowd was attracted to the exhibit, and the Woman's Club was highly praised for sponsoring such notable work. In the balcony of the club, however, was another exhibit, by members of the Studio Guild. Joan was one of two featured sculptors, and guests were encouraged to also visit the Guild's studio, still at 19 S.W. 2nd Street. Joan would find herself back at the Woman's Club at the end of February, for a one-week exhibit of fine paintings at the Woman's Club's

11th Annual Exhibit. While her best-known métier was sculpturing, Joan was significantly expanding her work in painting.

The Coral Gables Municipal Building was completed the week of March 5, 1939. Police and fire personnel had already been occupying the premises for several days when the City and WPA officials held a "house-warming" on March 17th. 50 guests in a holiday mood assembled in the small courtroom to hear Roy Schroder, the new WPA administrator for Florida, doing his first dedication since taking the position, present the gleaming new Municipal Building to the City. "This is one of the finest buildings in the state of Florida", Schroeder expressed his determination to make the federal agency a source of work and relief, proudly stating "It can be paralleled or duplicated in almost every county of the state. It is a standing example of what the WPA can and should do. It was not built by leaning on shovels."

Mayor Paul McGarry, accepting the building on behalf of the city, recalled that work on the building began exactly a year before, and spoke of Coral Gables' pride in the new building, a vivid contrast to "that dark, dilapidated, ramshackle place" a block away that had preceded it.

The only cloud over the evening were the imminent changes about to occur with the WPA. Schroder confirmed that WPA personnel in Florida would soon be drastically reduced because of recent drastic cuts in the appropriation for relief work throughout the country. Within weeks, The Works Progress Administration would become Work Projects Administration, and was placed under the new Federal Works Agency created on April 3rd. His words no doubt cast a pall over the evening. Of the 40,000 WPA employees in Florida alone, it was estimated that 4,000 to 8,000 jobs would be eliminated by April 8th, less than a month away.

After completing her work on the Municipal Building, Keller was far from idle. Sometime between late 1938 and early 1939, she began work on two busts, one of the antebellum songwriter Stephen Foster (1826-1864), the beloved "Father of American Music," who had wrote such classics as "Suwanee River", "Oh Susanna" and "My Old Kentucky Home") and one of Dr. John Gorrie (1803-1855), the inventor of artificial cooling, or

Stephen Foster

refrigeration. As Keller was not particularly known for such traditional work, these busts may have been commissioned by the National Youth Association, or perhaps at the prompting of her one-time mentor Lampert Bemelmans. In any event, her work was considered so outstanding that on April 16, 1939, headlines read *"Work of Ohio Girl Sculptor Will be Displayed At Fair"*. This was not referring to just any town fair – her work would be displayed to a multitude of visitors at the greatest fair in the United States – if not the world - showcased in the Florida House at The New York World's Fair of 1939, set to open its gates on April 30th.

ART BECOMES HER BEACON

Joan Keller is putting last touches on her bust of Stephen Foster, which has been accepted for exhibition in the Florida building of the New York World Fair.

Work Of Ohio Girl Sculptor Will Be Displayed At Fair

Keller Sculpting Her Foster Bust for the 1939 World's Fair

The concept of the fair had begun in four years earlier. At the height of the Great Depression, a group of New York businessmen came up with the concept of creating an international exposition. In 1935 they formed The New York World's Fair Corporation, with offices in the Empire State Building. Over the following four years the committee, which included such illustrious names as New York City Mayor Fiorello H. La Guardia and former Chief of Police Grover Whalen, who was named president of the corporation, planned, organized, and built the fair and exhibits.

The corporation entered into an agreement with the New York Park's Commissioner, securing a 1,216-acre site in Queens. They agreed to remove a vast ash dump and agreed the land would be permanently converted permanently into the Flushing Meadows-Corona Park at the

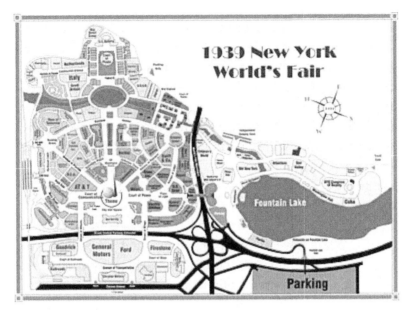

Map of the 1939 New York World's Fair

end of the exhibition. The overall theme selected for the fair was "Building the World of Tomorrow." It would become the second most expensive American world's fair to date, exceeded only by 1904's St. Louis' Louisiana Purchase Exposition. Promotion of the event had ramped up in earnest by 1938. The Brooklyn Dodgers, New York Giants and the Yankees all began wearing promotional patches on their uniforms, and the millionaire mogul and aviator Howard Hughes flew a special around-the-world flight to promote the extraordinary, enormous endeavor.

While the primary driving factor behind the fair was the goal of boosting US morale, and, more pragmatically, to lure sorely needed businesses into New York, it was agreed there should also be a cultural or historic association. Therefore, it was decided the opening would be held on the 150th anniversary of George Washington's first inauguration, which had taken place in lower Manhattan. The official colors of the fair were blue and orange. The wide avenues the stretched across the park were designed with a rich color scheme, which changed the further one walked from the center of the grounds. For example, the facilities along the Avenue of Pioneers were a progressive symphony of blue, starting with pale tints and eventually culminating in a deep, rich ultramarine. When the latest in lighting technology came on in the evenings, the effect was enchanting.

While several of the pavilions and other facilities were not yet completed, the Grand Opening took place as scheduled, with great pomp and circumstance, on a sweltering April 30, 1939. Dozens of foreign countries were represented, as well as such major national and international corporation as RCA, IBM, GM, Ford Motors and Westinghouse. Much attention was given to Westinghouse's Time capsule, which was not to opened for 5,000 years. It contained writings by Albert Einstein and Thomas Mann, copies of Life Magazine, a Mickey Mouse watch, a Gillette safety razor, a kewpie doll, a dollar in change, a pack of Camel cigarettes, millions of pages of various writings on microfilm and much more. Also sealed in the capsule were seeds for various crops, including wheat, corn, carrots, cotton and tobacco, all sealed in glass tubes. President Roosevelt delivered the opening remarks, which were not only heard over the radio, but were shown on over 200 of the newly developed televisions throughout the park.

On that first day, an estimated 206,000 visitors flocked to Flushing Meadows. Nearly 45,000,000 would eventually attend the fair. Divided into two seasons, the first

half of the exhibition ran from April 30, 1939 to October 31, 1939. After a six-month hiatus, the fair's second season opened on May 11, 1940 and ran through October 20th. General admission was 75 cents (almost $13.50 in 2021 values. Some exhibits had separate admission fees. If a visitor went to see all the attractions and included something to eat (there were several restaurants, ranging from casual to very upscale), it would not be unusual for a typical guest to spend $20.00 (roughly equivalent to $359.00 in 2021).

Florida House, 1939 New York World's Fair

Due to the size of the fair, it would not be unusual for people to make two or even three visits to see as much as possible.

Twenty-three states were represented at the fair. All of them, with the sole exception of Florida, were in the area dubbed the Court of States. Florida House was situated on the western shore of Fountain Lake in the Amusement Zone. At 110,000 square feet, it was by far the largest, and was more impressive than those housing the exhibitions of the other states – an impressive waterfront creation of a tropical paradise. The complex epitomized the architectural trends that had become synonymous with South Florida, replicating the Spanish-Mediterranean Revival style exemplified by Merrick and Mizner in such areas as Coral Gables and Palm Beach. The building's tower soared above the horizon, reminiscent of the magnificent towers which capped Coral Gables' Biltmore Hotel or the impressive Miami News building.

Equally impressive were the 45 exhibits lining the expansive walls of Florida House. They showcased the state's major points of interest, the advances in art, science and industry, and the state's abundant natural recreational resources. Florida House quickly became one of the 'must-see' spots to visit, and Joan's busts of Foster and Gorrie were frequently singled out for praise. Shortly after the first session of the fair closed on October 31, 1939, it would become apparent just how much her work had been appreciated.

Less than weeks after the intermission between the two sessions of the fair began, headlines in the Miami Herald informed their readers *WASHINGTON EXHIBIT TO GET FOSTER BUST – Work of Miami Artist To Be On Permanent Display in Capitol.*" Keller's work was so wildly acclaimed that Foster's bust had been taken to the headquarters of the National Youth Congress (also referred to as the American Youth Congress or the National Youth Administration) in Washington, D.C., where it had been placed on permanent display. Joan's work had been selected by directors of the Youth Congress after viewing it at the Florida House. The article also relayed some of her impressive credits: she had been on the staff of Lampert Bemelmans, and had exhibited at the Miami Art Center, the Four Arts Club in Palm Beach, and the Art Students League's exhibition in Miami.

Despite the strong support of First Lady Eleanor Roosevelt, who published a defense of the American Youth Congress entitled "Why I Still Believe in the Youth Congress", the Youth League would be disbanded the following year. Eventually its archives and holdings would be absorbed by the present-day General Services Administration. While this Keller bust of Stephen Foster may very well be tucked away somewhere in the dim vaults of the bowels of a GSA warehouse, its current whereabouts remains unknown.

While Joan was busy creating her Foster and Gorrie busts, members of her family were also keeping busy. Her handsome, only brother, John Joseph Keller, 26 and working as a house painter, married Rhoda Ashworth Edmonds (born March 25, 1919), the 20-year-old daughter of Arthur and Edith Edmunds, both natives of England. The couple wed at the Broward County Courthouse in Ft. Lauderdale on July 8, 1939. They began married life living with her parents in Miami, where her father owned a fire-wood yard. That left Joan the only unwed sibling in the family.

There was much more serious note in the nation that later summer of 1939. The tense situation in Europe was on the brink of exploding. Hitler's goal of an Aryan nation that would, in effect, control all of Europe was becoming less and less an abstract notion. Despite British Prime Minister's Neville Chamberlain's misguided confidence that war would be averted, combined with the continuing strong isolationist policy that characterized the United States, the world was still on edge. The fall from that precipice came on September 1, 1939, when Hitler invaded Poland. Two days later, with no recourse left to them, England and France both declared war on Germany, but, but for the time being they stood alone. While Roosevelt was sympathetic to the plight of his unprepared allies, the United States was going to continue neutral in what was essentially considered a European conflict.

While her brother was getting married and Europe was going to war, Keller was finishing a second Foster bust to replace the first at the World's Fair. It was created by Keller that summer, probably at the Gables Art & Architectural Building (still existing) at 2901 Ponce de Leon. George Merrick dubbed this area the Crafts Section, modeling it after a similar design for artisans and craftsmen in East Aurora, New York. Less likely is the suggestion that Joan did this work at the WPA's Coral Gables Art Center (which may, or may not, as will be demonstrated presently, have been the same building as the original Municipal Building and later the American Legion). It was noted that her instructor was Lampert Bemelmans. The second Foster bust was scheduled to make its public debut at the Homemaker Art Display, a WPA art exhibition at the chic Alcazar Hotel in downtown Miami.

Situated on prime real estate at 502 Biscayne Boulevard, the high-rise Alcazar (built in 1927, later demolished and currently the site of a parking lot for Miami-Dade College's Wolfson Campus), was a deluxe hotel,

Alcazar Hotel, Biscayne Blvd. Miami FL

famous for its glamorous cocktail lounge, and was adjacent to the towering Miami News Building. Built in 1925 and one of the city's most impressive buildings, the Miami News building would later become iconic as the Freedom Tower. During the uproar after Castro seized power in Cuba, it would become the first stop for thousands of fleeing Cuban refugees.

Interest was high for the Homemaker Art Display, and many column inches filled the newspapers in the days leading up to the two-hour exhibition, scheduled to be held on the mezzanine level of the Alcazar on the afternoon of November 24th. While open to the public, the Miami Daily News Homemaker Club dinner most definitely was not. The guest list headed by national and regional heads of the WPA,

Miami Mayor E.G. Sewell, the President of the Miami Chamber of Commerce, top management of the Miami Daily News, and some of the area's most noted artists, including Denman Fink. Joan's work was photographed, and she was featured in press photos with Lampert Bemelmans, so it is safe to assume that they were both among the elite guests.

Thus, is was on a high note that Joan stood, only four short years earlier a complete unknown amateur. As the 1930s drew to a close, she was one of the most recognized and lauded young artists of her generation. It seemed highly probable that the next decade would see her bloom into a major figure in the highly competitive school of fine art. Unbeknownst to her, the limelight she was basking in would dramatically change with an experience that led to a rude awakening.

Miami News Tower, Currently known as the Miami Freedom Tower

CHAPTER 5
AT A CROSSROADS –
MIAMI, 1940-1942

AT A CROSSROADS – MIAMI, 1940-1942

The first six months of 1940 were relatively quiet for Keller. A request was submitted in 2018 for any information pertaining to her to the National Archives Records Administration (NARA), which holds the surviving records of the Federal Arts Project division. The scope of their holdings is immense, with tens of thousands of documents ranging from historical documents to trivial notes. A search of files that dealt specifically with personnel records produced but a single document, a memorandum from a Thomas C. Parker to a Mr. C.E. Triggs dated March 19, 1940. It reads:

"With reference to your memorandum of March 5 concerning human interest material which Mrs. Kerr feels would be of interest to Mr. Carmody, I am attaching a card, in triplicate, with a photograph, for this purpose.

"The subject, Joan Keller, started in the sculpture classes of the Miami Art Center and without other instruction has developed into a promising young artist.

"Additional copies of the photographs are available, if required."

The identities of the Parker, Triggs and Carmoody mentioned in this memo are unknown. The referenced memo of March 5th is not in the file, nor is the photograph.

In June, a soft article in the Miami Herald resumed covering her activities. Joan was said to still be living at 231 NW 24 Avenue, although no record of her could be located in the 1940 US census. Perhaps. as some of her work was being displayed in Washington, D.C. at the time, she was somehow missed by the census takers.

The Herald reported that Keller *"is a local sculptress who takes her art seriously and is meeting with great success.*

Keller Home NW 24th Ave, 1940

"She did a bust of a Seminole Indian, chiseled in limestone, which is being exhibited in Washington where is receiving flattering attention. In Washington also, at the headquarters of the National Youth Congress Miss Keller has a bust of Stephen Foster which is getting its share of popular acclaim. She has on exhibition at this time in the Florida exhibit at the World's Fair in New York an over life size bust of Stephen Foster.

"At the Adriene-Ardis Art Gallery in Miami, Miss Keller has a cast stone man's figure which is called 'Despair.'

"The above works and others which have been seen here, have caused Miss Keller's friends among Miami artists to say that she has a depth of perception and a mastery of technique which make her outstanding in the world of art. And she is young too. And most attractive."

The above mentioned "Despair" sculpture, hewn from stone, was a rare example of Joan sculpting a life-size work that was deemed *"so indicative of the mood that the name of the piece is self-evident."*

That September, Joan held what was apparently her first one-person exhibit at the Coral Gables Art Center on Salzedo. Of the twelve pieces of sculpture on display, the most notable was a head of Frederick A. Delano, Chairman of the National Resources Planning Board and uncle of President Roosevelt. The Delano bust was to be sent to Tallahassee for the office of George G. Gross, Executive Secretary of the State Planning Board.

News coverage of the exhibit stated that Joan was a guest at the recent Florida Day at the New York World's Fair, where her second Stephen Foster bust was on display, adding *"Miss Keller, who formerly worked with the Florida Art Project's sculpture unit, now is continuing her studies in New York."* It was the first indication that Joan was leaving Florida for the brighter, wider world of Manhattan.

Whether Joan had already relocated to New York by September 1940 is questionable. On one hand, no mention could be found in the South Florida media about her for the next year. The next major event in her life that has been discovered occurred nearly a year later. However, that article, datelined September 7, 1941, references an event that had occurred six months earlier – an event that possibly came close to ending her life and probably changed her, possibly both physically and emotionally in several ways.

On April 16th (or 19th ; the same article references both dates), Joan was at work in her Coral Gables studio at the Art & Architectural Building. She was

2901 Ponce de Leon Blvd

in the small rotunda of the building when she took a fall over the bannister and then hurdled down three flights of the winding staircase. Luckily, she wasn't killed, but she broke

her back and was in serious condition for what appears to be several months. While recuperating, she lived with her aunt, Florence King.

What is intriguing about this is that in the 1940 US Census, Richard Merrick, noted as a single art instructor, listed the same address as his residence. Richard had been married in 1932 to Marion Wallace, but the couple had divorced in 1936. Without speculating, it is interesting that the commercial

Richard Merrick

building Richard listed as his home was at the same address as Joan's studio less than a year later.

Sculptor Continues Work, Ignoring Broken Back

Miss Joan Keller Does Scale Model For School Fountain While Convalescing

Despite her condition, with her leg still in a cast and her back strapped, by September Joan was back at work, making a scale model for a fountain to be placed in a Dade County School. The school was unnamed in the press, and searches at Coral Gables elementary and middle schools have proven fruitless.

The September 17th article continued, *"To the healthy indolent, such ambition may seem unusual. However, judging from Miss Keller's youthful appearance, and the amount of work she has done in a short lifetime, she finds this one job much too little to be doing, and the event of her accident a serious handicap to her output. She will be back in her studio as soon as her cast is removed.*

"Now Ms. Keller, who came to Miami six years ago, is one of the few sculptors who hew directly from rock. Most of them have turned to modeling in clay, then having their work chiseled by machine from the rock. Miss Keller blocks roughly on the rock in charcoal. This assists her in locating the masses of her work. From then on, she uses tools, chiseling by hand.

"She works for the W.P.A., with which she has been connected for four years. She has done a series of Seminoles from pictures, though she feels it is much better to have a model. One of these heads went to Washington and is now on a traveling exhibit.

What Joan would have preferred most in her professional life was the privilege of modeling her own creations. While her commissions and assignments at the time show great empathy and make her work seem complete, it was when she chose her subject that her sculpture took on an added warmth and humanity.

Perhaps the best example of this added dimension was the plaster head she did around this time of the famous artist and sculptor Henri Gaudier-Brzeska (1891-1915). Gaudier, whose work as a sculptor displayed a rough-hewn, almost primitive, style of direct carving, making it clear she drew no small degree of inspiration from his work. While photographs of the compelling work attest to its artistry, the survival, or the present whereabouts of this homage to her posthumous mentor, is unknown.

Gaudier, a native of Orleans, France, was 19 when he moved to London in 1910, with the goal of becoming an artist (like Joan, he had no formal training of any real significance when he started his career). He was soon associated with Vorticism, a literary and artistic movement that briefly flourished in England from 1912 until 1915. Vorticism, opposed, indeed scorned, 19th century sentimentality, landscapes and nudes, instead relating art to industrialization and extolling the energy of machine and machine-made products. Vorticist compositions were sharped planed (also characteristic of Joan) and revealed elements of its origins in Cubism (from which it was derived) and Futurism movements (with which is more closely related, embracing dynamism, all things modern and bold lines). The genre was taking root by 1912, and it became official when a group of artists broke away from their contemporaries and signed the Vorticist Manifesto in 1914.

Henri Gaudier-Brzeska

Also, like Joan, Gaudier soon focused his talents almost exclusively on sculpting. He was a rising star when the Great War erupted, and he enlisted in the French Army. Less than a year later, he was killed in the trenches at Neuville-Saint-Vaast. He was only 23. His brief career had lasted only four years – another parallel to Joan's limited time of major prominence. Joan had admired his work, which was displayed at such famed venerable museums as the Tate for many years. Joan sculpted the Gaudier head simply because she was inspired to do so.

Joan continued to work steadily during 1940 and 1941, until she was sidelined by her accident. There was a self-portrait, using mirrors to capture every angle. The socially prominent Ethel E. Murrell, wife of well-known attorney John M. Murrell, of 1500 Brickell Avenue (in the days when Brickell Avenue was still primarily residential,) was the subject of a bronze-finish plaster work depicting three heads, each depicting a different mood, which took three sittings. A scale plaster model of a Seminole Indian with a fishing spear, done for the Coral Gables Chamber of Commerce, was displayed at the art center in Key West, while a study of hands was crafted from Texas limestone. Keller also did a series of both male and female Seminole busts for the WPA, chiseled by hand.

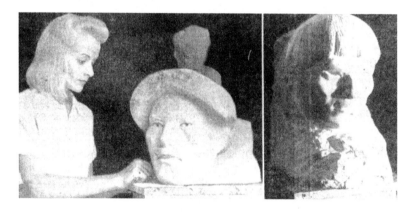

The lengthy article from the Miami Daily News that lauded her for continuing her work despite the serious injuries she had sustained, concluded *"The modern manner, represented by Ponce de Leon in a suit of armor, the classical feeling, evident in most of Miss Keller's head and busts, civic motifs, used in several group works, native busts of Seminoles, all indicate the adaptability of this artist's flexible fingers"*.

Two months later, on Sunday, December 7, 1941, the East Coast of the United States was just sitting down to lunch when telegraph lines and radios went into frantic overdrive, bearing the first news that Japan had attacked Pearl Harbor. While initial reports had 300 dead in Hawaii, the toll of fatalities would rapidly climb to over 2,400. Over 200 Naval personnel, 109 marines, 218 from the US Army as well at 68 civilians. Of the total of 2,403 souls who perished that day, 1,177, nearly half, were from the USS Arizona.

Those who had paid attention to the world's volatility over recent months were not shocked over the assault, but for most citizens it was inconceivable that Imperial Japan had indeed crossed an irreversible boundary into war. Frantic for news – any news – America was galvanized into action. Even die-hard isolationists scrambled to  pledge complete support to President Roosevelt as Commander-in-Chief. The following day, Roosevelt, delivered with steady voice and firm conviction his "A Day That Will Live in Infamy" speech, requested and received from Congress a Declaration of War against Japan, Germany, and Italy.

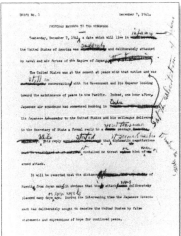

While the public did not realize it, the USA was headed straight out of the lingering Depression. America mobilized, and as men and women found jobs, a biproduct of the mobilization would be the eventual dismantling of the WPA. It can be argued that deadly December day marked, if initially only symbolically, the end of the Great Depression.

One would have thought Joan would be returning to her promising career full time shortly. One would have thought wrong. For whatever reason, Joan departed Miami to live in New York. She left not only Miami, she also walked away from her sculpting career and decided to go down a completely different path.

SCULPTRESS FORGOTTEN

CHAPTER 6

A NEW CAREER, MARRIAGE & MOTHERHOOD, NEW YORK, 1942-1949

A NEW CAREER, MARRIAGE &
MOTHERHOOD, NEW YORK, 1942-1949

While the reports of Joan moving to New York City by September 1941 were apparently premature, it seems that she did make the permanent move sometime in the late fall of 1941 or early winter of 1942. While it does not appear that she extended any great effort on her art, but she was seeming considering a completely new career, of which more shortly.

While Joan was presumably focused on exploring a new career in New York or was perhaps pondering which direction to take with her future, there were also new developments within her close-knit family. By 1943 she was the aunt of a two-year old nephew, John Edmonds Keller, born to her brother John and wife Rhoda in Miami on August 7, 1941. Her youngest sister Margaret and her husband Raymond (Russell) Washburn also ended their five-year marriage in 1943. The couple, who had no children, may have already been separated for a period. When Raymond enlisted as a private at Camp Blanding, near Starke, FL, he stated he had completed two years of college, was married, lived in Fort Lauderdale, where he was employed as a manager at Home Lumber and Supply Company. Raymond signed up for "the duration of the war or other emergency, plus six months, subject to the discretion of the President or otherwise according to law." In his draft card records, his personal information is virtually identical, except that he stated his next of kin was "R. Washburn," who he identified as his wife, not Margaret. Russell lived in Fort Lauderdale from at least 1942 to 1958, and probably longer. A very brief obituary noted his death, aged 75, in Broward County on

February 24, 1987. There was no mention of any survivors and the notice indicates he was cremated.

1944 would be a tragic year for the Keller family. Four years earlier, on November 11, 1940, John Keller, who was working as a contractor in Miami, had joined the National Guard, remaining after the war began a year later. In July 1942 he transferred to parachute school at Fort Benning, GA, and was initially assigned to the new 507th Parachute Infantry Regiment, founded at Camp Toccoa, GA that same month under the 82nd Airborne Division. In July 1943 John was granted furlough to see his family in Miami. As Joan was living in New York, its unknown if she was able to go south to see her brother and infant nephew.

Returning to Europe, John rejoined the 507th, soon to be nicknamed "Raff's Ruffians," which arrived in Ireland and England in December 1943 to prepare for their first major mission, an action which would help alter the course of the war. Their task that spring of 1944 was named "Mission Boston," part of the Allied airborne landings in Normandy. To the world, the day of the invasion, June 6th, would become forever known as D-Day. Their target was Amfreville, but confusion caused by heavy cloud cover resulted in a widely scattered landing by the 507th. John, by then Captain Keller, and other members of the division, who had parachuted behind the German lines, continued to fight in the Battle of Normandy. In two long days, the 507th lost nearly 200 men before being withdrawn and returned to England.

In the frenzied haste of the evacuations, the whereabouts and condition of John was unknown. For a tortured month, despite increasingly desperate entreaties, the Keller family had no word of him. It was not until July 10th that the War Department informed his wife Rhoda, at her home at 3516 NW 19th Avenue in Miami, that her husband had been killed in action on June 16th, ten days after the assault had begun. John was 29 years old. In addition to his widow, son and mother, he was survived by his three sisters, Julia Brickman (of Hialeah) and Joan and Margaret Keller (both of New York). Margaret had apparently reverted to her maiden name after her divorce from Russell Washburn the previous year. He was also survived by two aunts, Florence King and Mrs. John Woods, both of Miami. John was initially buried in St. Mere Egilse in Normandy. At the end of the war, the burial site was removed to Omaha Beach. Rhoda requested her husband's remains be returned to the United States.

On July 27, 1943, President Franklin Roosevelt, "on behalf of a grateful nation," bestowed posthumously upon John the Purple Heart medal, second only the Medal of Honor decoration as the highest recognition of valor four wounds or death suffered in combat. John was also awarded the Honorable Service World War II "Ruptured Duck" lapel pin, the American Defense Medal, awarded for being on active duty between December 8, 1939 and June 7, 1941, and the Victory Medal World War II, awarded for being on active duty between December 7, 1941 and December 31, 1946.

THE SECRETARY OF WAR
WASHINGTON

July 27, 1944.

My dear Mrs. Keller:

    At the request of the President, I write to inform you that the Purple Heart has been awarded posthumously to your husband, Captain John J. Keller, Infantry, who sacrificed his life in defense of his country.

    Little that we can do or say will console you for the death of your loved one. We profoundly appreciate the greatness of your loss, for in a very real sense the loss suffered by any of us in this battle for our country, is a loss shared by all of us. When the medal, which you will shortly receive, reaches you, I want you to know that with it goes my sincerest sympathy, and the hope that time and the victory of our cause will finally lighten the burden of your grief.

               Sincerely yours,

               Henry L. Stimson

Mrs. Rhoda A. Keller,
    3516 N. W. 10th Avenue,
    Miami, Florida.

1944   Letter from Henry Stimson, Secretary of War to Rhoda Edmonds Keller
               Purple Heart awarded Captain John J. Keller
                   3516 NW 10th Ave., Miami, FL
                       July 27, 1944

As grateful as the Keller family was for these honors and posthumous awards, the healing process could not really progress until John's remains were returned home. The family was finally able to bury John in his home soil on May 28, 1948, nearly four years after his death. Cleveland's Plain Dealer newspaper of May 25th announced the family would receive friends at the Wm. L. Wagner & Son Funeral Home at 1951 E. 75th Street, near Euclid. Funeral services took place at St. Ann's Church, located at Cedar and Coventry Rd. on the morning of the 28th, with full military honors under the direction of V.F.W. Post 3445, with burial at Calvary Cemetery. Per his burial notice, Joan was married and referred to as Mrs. Theresa Joan Louie of the Bronx, NY. Her sister Margaret had remarried and was named as Mrs. Margaret Clark McGuire of New York City. On the same day as his burial, John's widow Rhoda signed the government application for a flat granite tombstone to mark his final resting place. The application was duly approved on August 7th, and the simple marker remains there to this day.

Margaret's second husband was James Clark McGuire, native of Washington, D.C. 20 years her senior, having been born April 17. 1896. He had enlisted in the US Armed Forces May 28, 1917, serving until May 20, 1919.

By 1940 he had been married and divorced, and was living in New York City, where he was employed by the Port Authority. The couple were living in New York at the same time as Joan, who at the time of Margaret's remarriage, was the only one of the Keller sisters who had not yet married.

Margaret, Mary Jane, Tess, Nana
Florida – Circa 1940's

On January 30, 1945, at age 28, Joan quietly married King Wair Louie (sometimes referred to as John King Louie.) King was born in Sunning, China, December 3, 1917. When he first arrived in the US is unclear. What is known is that at age 12 he departed from China, noted as his last place of residence, sailing from Hong Kong aboard the USS President McKinley and arriving in Seattle in December 1929.

According to an affidavit by his father, Louie was already a US citizen and was a student. He obviously had returned to China at least once. The US Government Index to Chinese Exclusion Case Files, which documented re-entry by Chinese nationals and US citizens of Chinese ancestry to the US, recorded his name as King Wai Louie. Some curious facts emerge from this 1939 case file. King, aged 19, was noted as being from Sun Suey, Toishan Province, China. For reason he had used the alias Gar Theu Louie and underwent a lengthy interrogation by authorities for reasons unstated. Under "Occupation" was written "Citizen's Return," which confirms his citizenship status. However, the question is raised as to why he would have required a sponsor, in his case someone by the name of Sun Kwong On. King gave his address as 55 Mott Street, New York. Located in Chinatown, the tenement building at this address was still standing in 2018.

59 Mott Street, New York City

It is not known when King moved to New York, where he married Keller six months after her brother John's death. Joan did assume his surname, and going forward was referred to as Jon Keller Louie, or just as frequently, as Jon Louie Keller. Occasionally it was simply Jon Louie. It should be noted that the name "Joan" also disappears around this time, replaced by the typically masculine name "Jon." As for King, he apparently informally used the first name John (perhaps in honor of his wife, her father and late brother), but he appears to have used it infrequently.

Anecdotal evidence and a handful of 8x10 glamor shots lend credence to the fact, however unlikely at first glance she turned onto a new career path – that of becoming a high-fashion model. And while New York City was home to scores of modeling agencies and struggling models, Joan, who was possibly modeling before her marriage either started, or else soon moved right to the top tier, working for the relatively new Conover Model Agency, already deemed a rising powerhouse in the field. She was clearly working for Conover by 1945. That year her name was penciled as "Jon Louie" on the back of a glamour shot stamped "Harry Conover," although it is possible, she had joined the agency before marrying King. A second, undated penciled notation on the back read "Jon (Louie) Keller" and "Conover Model in her youth." The same photo notes her as having blonde hair, blue eyes, 5'7 1/2," and her measurements being 33-22-34. A relative recalled Joan walked with a slight limp, the result of a fall when she was a child in Cleveland, but even so he related "she seemed to float or glide along with grace." Her new career could be deemed successful, with her photo appearing in many of the national glossy fashion magazines that dominated the fashion field. Unless one was a major star in the fashion or another field, however, models seldom were credited by name.

A Chicago native, Joan's new boss, Harry S. Conover, was a raffish, good-looking young man who came to New York about 1931 and soon secured a modeling job for the prestigious John Robert Powers Agency. Tall, with green eyes and wavy hair (he would later be named one of the country's "Best Dressed Men" by the Fashion Foundation of America), for eight years Conover enjoyed a moderate degree of success as a model. While at Powers, he became friends with fellow model Gerald Ford (the future President of the United States.) When Conover realized "there was more money at the top" and decided to open his own agency, Ford was persuaded by model Phyllis Brown to

Harry Conover in his office, age 28, 1939

invest $1,000 in the new venture, becoming Conover's silent partner. The Harry Conover Modeling Agency quickly became one of the "Big Three" modeling agencies in the country, together with his former employer John Robert Powers and Walter Thornton. Conover was only 28 years old.

Credited with coining the term "Cover Girl", the Conover firm was soon grossing over $2,000,000 a year. Instead of the breed of svelte, paper-thin mannequins then in vogue, he instead promoted what he called "the kind of natural, well-scrubbed girl you used to take to the junior prom." With his showmanship and charm he had little difficulty placing his models on the cover of the country's most popular magazines. "Eat as much as you want," he would tell his staff of several hundred models as WWII drew to an end, adding "returning servicemen want a good, well-rounded bundle, not a matchstick".

Jon Keller Louie "Tess"
Revlon Nail Polish Display, Miami, FL
July 10, 1956

In 1941, Conover discussed his promotion of the natural look. "Over 75 percent of our appointments today are made for the well-scrubbed American girl business. This demands a new type of girl – one whom we call 'vitaluring.' Interestingly enough, she has the same type of personality and looks that has always been demanded of men models. Men have always had to look like Ralph, the boy next door. Today's girls must look like Ruth, Ralph's sister. This doesn't mean that they may not look sophisticated. But it must be a real sophistication, one that comes from within instead of one that is painted on."

While it is not known how he came to meet Joan, Conover found many of his "typical American girls" through scouts posted in such venues as college campuses and festival queens culled from universities across the country. Joan, at 25, was a bit older than these co-eds, but she had always looked younger than her age.

As part of his "de-glamorizing" his girls from the sleek, gaunt fashion images that had reigned until his arrival, he frequently changed their names to such playful, cute (and memorable) tags as Choo-Choo Johnson, Frosty Webb, Chili Williams and Dulcet Tone. These name changes also served another purpose. As Conover saw it, these unusual names would often cause photographers to ask specifically for the young women by their new names. With any luck, the photographers would remember Choo Choo, Frosty or Chili and call on them for future work. In essence, he introduced the 'Star System' of film into the modeling world. It was exactly what the studios had been doing for over 40 years, and it worked just as well. A number of his models went on to Hollywood, where they worked with varying degrees of success, including Constance Ford, Anita Colby, Joan Caufield and Jinx Falkenberg…and of course the tag line "Cover Girl" would become famous world-wide when Rita Hayworth starred in a smash hit of the same name in 1944. While Hayworth never worked for Conover, two others in the cast and crew, Anita Colby and Jinx Falkenberg, were Conover Cover Girls.

There is no question that Joan, despite being a little older than the typical model, completely embodied the essence of what Conover was seeking. Without appearing artificial or overly made-up, she was a beautiful teenager who evolved into a stunningly attractive woman, with that hard-to-define naturalness that once seen, was rarely forgotten. In some photos, she reminds one of Carole

Lombard, film star wife of Clark Gable, who died too young when she was killed in a horrific plane crash following a US Bond tour in January 1942 in the first weeks of War II.

However, in her Conover years, whether by accident or design, Joan bears an undeniable resemblance to Paramount's diminutive Veronica Lake, 20 years old in 1942, a rising star often teamed with Alan Ladd. Lake's long blonde hair, with peek-a-boo bangs which tended to fall over one eye, was her trademark. The hairstyle that defined her became a hazard when women working in the defense industry would get their peak-a-boo tresses caught in the machinery, causing injuries, not only to the defense workers but to the machinery. The government stepped in and Paramount coerced Lake to pose for publicity photos in which she reacted painfully to her hair getting caught in a drill press to heighten awareness about her hazardous hairstyle. The following year a Paramount newsreel, filmed at the behest of the War Womanpower Commission shows a chastened Lake in an upswept hairdo to discourage her dangerous bangs being copied by the 'Rosie the Riveter' workforce. While doubtless part studio hype and part reality, in Tinsel Town it was generally thought that losing her bangs also caused Lake's career to also lose its momentum. This was the era that created the pin-up girl, primarily movie stars and starlets, ranging from Betty Grable and Dorothy Lamour to emerging models like Norma Jeanne Baker, who would emerge by the beginning of the next decade as one of Hollywood's most enduring icons under the name of Marilyn Monroe. Tellingly, Monroe was 10 years younger, and seemingly far more ambitious than Keller.

Jinx Falkenburg

Choo Choo Johnson

Chili Williams

Anita Colby

Bevy of Beauties

Some of Keller's Fellow Models at Conover

Within three months of their marriage, the USA was finally close to ending the War that had consumed the country and taken the lives of so many in service on fronts from Japan to Europe. The Battle of Okinawa, which began April 1, 1945 (and did not end for almost two months), took 82,000 casualties. Less than two weeks later, the nation was grief-stricken and stunned when President Roosevelt, who had just been sworn in for his fourth term as head of the nation in January, died at his retreat in Warm Springs, GA on April 11th. Thousands of men with doffed hats, and tearful women lined the railways from Georgia to Washington to pay tribute to the funeral cortege of the man who had guided them from the depth of the Great Depression, only to face a world war unprecedented in scope. Vice President Harry Truman became the Commander in Chief, determined to complete Roosevelt's goal, and end the conflicts on both fronts once and for all.

The end of the war was in sight. As the Allied Forces converged on Berlin, on April 30, Hitler committed suicide in his bunker in the German capitol. A week later, the German military surrender was signed at Reims, which the Allies accepted the following day. It was May 8, 1945, Truman's 61st birthday, but would become better known as V-E Day. The President, who had been in office for a mere three weeks, dedicated the victory to the memory of the late Roosevelt. He decreed that flags which had been at half-staff remain so for the duration of the 30 days of official mourning, and stated his only wish was that Roosevelt "had lived to witness this day. Despite being in deep mourning, massive celebrations took place across the country, especially in New York's Time Square.

With Germany and Italy vanquished, the USA could concentrate on Japan. With the completion of the atomic bomb, the Potsdam Declaration was issued on July 6, with Truman bluntly telling Japan to "Surrender or suffer prompt and utter destruction." A belligerent Japan rejected the ultimatum three days later. Truman wasn't bluffing. On August 6, the US dropped the atomic bomb known as "Little Boy" on Hiroshima, leaving anywhere between 65,000 and 200,000 dead. Sixteen hours later, Truman warned Japan one last time, stating that if they did not surrender, they could "expect a rain of ruin from the air, the like of which has never been seen on this earth."

For three days, Americans held their breath and stayed glued to their radios. Good to his word, Truman ordered a second bomb, named "Fat Man", this one devasting Nagasaki and killing another 39,000 to 80,000. The following day, August 10th, Emperor Hirohito caved in and the Japanese Foreign Ministry notified the Allies through Swiss channels of their intention to surrender, provided Hirohito retained his throne. News of the offer was

enough to start the celebrations in earnest, with American soldiers in Berlin shouting "It's over in the Pacific!" The Allies notified their willingness to accept Japan's terms.

On August 14 (August 15 in Japan), the Allied Governments announced Japan's surrender and the date would forever be known as V-J Day. Truman was scheduled to address the nation at 7PM. However, as the news came out of the Japanese acceptance of defeat, but before Truman spoke to a jubilant nation, American's began celebrating "as if joy had been rationed and saved up for three years, eight months and seven days since December 7, 1941." As crowds and celebratory demonstrations commenced across the country, New York City went mad with elation, with the largest crowd in the history of Times Square beyond giddy that at last the nightmare, despite the sickening loss of so many of what would become known as "The Greatest Generation" was finally over. It was later said that night sparked a coast-to-coast frenzy of servicemen "kissing everyone in skirts that happened along." There would be time enough in the days, weeks and months to come to mourn the empty chairs in the dining room, the sadness of babies who would grow up never knowing their fathers, and the countless widows and sweethearts who would never again see the men they had loved and lost.

As the country was beginning to come to terms with the new post-war world, Cyril Brickman, the husband of Joan's sister Julia, died of spinal meningitis, for which there then was no cure, in a Miami hospital on Valentine's Day 1946, at the age of 33, a month shy of his 34th birthday. It will be recalled that it had been Brickman and his close friend, Joan's late brother John, had been the first of the family to leave Cleveland and head south to Miami 11 years earlier. His 10-year marriage to Julia had produced six sons in rapid succession – George (Guy), John (Jack), William (Bill), Patrick (Pat), Michael (Mike) and Richard (Dick), the last little more than an infant when Cyril died. He had registered for the draft in Miami on October 16, 1940, but according to descendants, didn't see active service. A marine hardware buyer, Brickman was a member of St, John's Apostle Church in Hialeah. Following a Requiem Mass at St. Mary's Catholic Church, Brickman was buried at Woodlawn Park Cemetery, leaving the still young Julia a widow with six young boys. On the same day, February 16, when Cyril was buried, Joan gave birth to her first child, Marie, by all accounts a beautiful baby.

The remaining years of the 1940s appear to have been quiet for Joan, King Louie and little Marie, and by 1949 the family had returned to Miami. The reason behind their return is unknown. The 1949 Miami City Directory shows Louie and Joan (using the name Jon) living at 75 W. 24 Street. Louie found work as a waiter at the Cathay House, apparently a restaurant. Joan's career with Conover had paid the bills, but aside from a handful of glossy PR photos, it seems clear she had never had the drive or the passion, despite her beauty, to be a glamorized cover girl or gain fame for capturing the imagination of the public simply on the base of her pin-up looks. Leave that to Veronica Lake, Dorothy Lamour and even Marilyn Monroe. It seems certain that Keller was returning to Miami to rekindle her art career. How successful that would be was the question mark.

CHAPTER 7
SECOND CHANCE,
MIAMI, 1950-1960

SECOND CHANCE, MIAMI, 1950-1960

The Miami Keller returned to in 1949 was dramatically different from the one she had left at the outset of the War. In 1940, the population of Dade County was just over 170,000. Though many cities and towns were heavily affected by the conflict, Miami had remained relatively unscathed. Instead of building large army and naval bases to train the men going off to war, the Army and Navy instead came to South Florida, converting hotels to barracks, movie theaters to classrooms and local beaches and golf courses into training grounds. Overall, more than 500,000 enlisted men and 50,000 officers were trained in South Florida. When the war ended many servicemen and women returned to Miami, with the result that by 1950, the population had risen to in excess of 500,000.

In Coral Gables, control of the famed Biltmore Hotel, George Merrick's masterpiece, had been assumed by the Government and converted into an Army Air Force hospital. The property had been sold to the Government for $895,000, which included the hotel, the country club ballroom, the north golf course and over 165 acres of land, It took over 70 pages alone to inventory the furnishings, fixtures and other real property that were included in the transaction. After the war, the VA acquired the property, which would remain a medical facility until 1969, when it relocated to a new building near Jackson Memorial. When Keller returned, she would no longer attend swank parties or swim in the famous pool of the former hotel that had briefly and gloriously been the crown jewel of the City Beautiful.

Coral Gables and Miami had changed in other ways by the time Joan returned. Having spent the first years of her career under the auspices of the WPA, where she had flourished, she could not return to the roots that had nurtured her and made her famous. After the outbreak of the war, jobs quickly became plentiful for both men and women and the WPA, which had helped the country survive the Depression, had been dissolved in June 1943.

Keller was not only returning to a different town, but one she would be attempting to reconquer alone. Some of her most valuable contacts from the 1930s were either dead or in declining health. Denman Fink, George Merrick's architectural genius was by then 70 and would soon retire from the University of Miami's Art Department and live out his final years at the Floridean Rest Home (still standing at 47 NW 32 Place) with his wife Zillah until his death from a stroke in June 1956. He was cremated and buried at Woodlawn.

Phineas Paist   *Richard Merrick*

Richard Merrick, an important colleague of Keller's, and George Merrick's youngest sibling was a very prominent artist and instructor in his own right. His and Joan's paths had crossed frequently during the Depression era. In 1940, he was single and, as noted above, was living at 2901 Ponce de Leon Blvd, the same address given as the location of Keller's studio, where she had suffered the fall that had nearly taken her life. In any event, the relationship between Merrick and Keller will probably never be known for certain. By 1950, Keller was married, but Richard remained a bachelor until 1959, when he wed Mildred Heath Selle, a marriage which lasted until his death in 1986.

Perhaps the most important person who had guided her career was the rather mysterious Lampert Bemelmans, whose rather sketchy past has been recounted above. Bemelmans, with his wife Emma, is listed in the Miami City Directories consistently from the early 1930s through 1945, with his occupation noted as sculptor, after which the path grows cold.

By the late fall of 1949. Keller was again pregnant, and at Victoria Hospital on June 22, 1950, she gave birth to a son, Kenneth Alexis Louie. A month later, on July 29th, her sister Julia Brickman, widowed by Cyril Brickman four years earlier, married Vincent DePaul (Vinny) Gillen, at St. John the Apostle Church, 479 E. 4 Street, Hialeah – the same church where she and Brickman had been members, A surviving wedding photograph shows a beaming Julia in a light suit, gloves, a halo straw hat and spectator pumps, surrounded, among others, in the front row by her new husband, three of her six sons, her aunt, Florence King, and her niece Marie. In the second row, with a white mantilla head covering, eyes downcast and blonde hair shining, is an enigmatic and stunningly lovely Joan, looking remarkably like the late film star Carole Lombard. Altogether over 25 people are posed in the photograph, and one could easily overlook the partially hidden face of a shorter man with receding black hair. It was only in 2018 that, thanks to one of Joan's Brickman nephews that he was identified as King Louie. It is one of the only photographs of him that has been seen by these researchers.

Vincent Gillen was born in Ozone Park, NY, on June 6, 1914, and was raised in Queens, where he lived until at least 1940. After finishing two years of high school he became a skilled chauffeur, and was licensed to drive a bus, taxi, truck, or tractor. Gillen was single and without dependents when, in Jamaica, NY he enlisted as a private with the Warrant Officers, USA, on April 24, 1941, seven months before Pearl Harbor. When he came to Miami is not known, but he was presumably living at the hotel/boarding house that Cyril Brickman had built adjacent to the Hialeah Race Track to not only to provide a home for his growing family, but also generate income from boarders and guests, and where Gillen met Julia. On July 26, 1950, Vincent, identified as a carpenter's helper, and Julia filed an application to wed, which they did three days later.

Wedding Photo, Julia Keller Brickman Gillen & Vincent Gillen
St. John the Apostle Church, 479 E. 4ᵗʰ Street, Hialeah, FL
July 29, 1950

To put Joan's professional career at the time in perspective, it is necessary to regress for a moment, to August 1949. On August 7ᵗʰ, the newspapers reported that the Tucker Art Gallery would be opening its doors at 3917 Alton Road, Miami Beach, on or about November 1ˢᵗ. The aim of new gallery was to display the works of contemporary European artists which had not been seen in this country since the winds of war began in earnest in 1939, as well as paintings by local artists. The plan for establishing the gallery were established by Eve Tucker after her return from Europe, where she had served as administration officer of the Restitution of Art Works Program for Austria, which was headquartered in Vienna.

Jon Keller Louie (Tess)
On Roof over the Wash Room
75 W. 24th Street, Hialeah, FL
Circa 1950's

After the dust had settled when the war ended, work had entered a new stage for the Monuments, Fine Arts & Archives (MFAA) Section of the US Army's Civil Affairs Division, which became popularly known as "The Monuments Men" (which in 2014 was very adapted into a quite successful film, starring George Clooney (who also directed), Matt Damon, Bill Murray and John Goodman). The Section was comprised of a select group of handpicked art historians, architects, archivists, artists and curators culled from some of the country's finest cultural institutions. Their goal was to locate, preserve, protect the massive amounts of artwork which had been plundered by the Nazi regime and return these works, some of which were of incalculable value, to the countries from which they had been seized.

However, what is not generally known is that while the vast majority of these experts were men, there were a small number of women who were equally instrumental in this mission. One of the most important of these was Evelyn Tucker (1906-1996). A graduate of the University of Miami, she joined the Women's Army Corps. At the war's end, she was assigned to the MFAA, initially as an Administrative Assistant and then as Fine Arts Director, serving in the latter position from March to July 1946, and from October 1947 to February 1949.

Tucker's Herculean task consisted of returning 400 tons of art that had been commandeered by the Nazis and secreted in the Alt Aussie Salt Mine near Salzburg. By the time she returned to the States, she was well-known in art circles, having lectured extensively on her work in Austria. The Miami News, in announcing the gallery's opening, noted "With the difficult job of restoring the old masters came many associations and also many opportunities to observe what is being done by today's artists on the continent...filled with enthusiasm and knowledge gleaned from her work and associations, Miss Tucker has succeeded in establishing her gallery." She would relocate to New Mexico, where she would live until her death in 1996.

Eve Tucker

Tucker's professional association with Keller came shortly after the new year. On January 15, 1950, the galleries announced that a one-man showing of works by Keller, referred to as Jon Louie Keller, would begin on the 17th and run through the end of the month. To avoid confusion, it was clarified that she was better known in art circles as Joan Keller, adding that "her recent work, which consists of paintings, sculpture and ceramics, has oriental flavor and a highly original quality." In other words, Keller's latest creations were evolving from the Depression era of stark, chiseled lines and, with her work taking on a new, more contemporary appearance. It would mark her first professional reappearance on the Miami art scene "after several years absence".

Keller's Ceramic Figures

Moving away from the sculptures which had made her name, Keller was not only returning to painting, but also expanding into ceramics. A few days after the opening, an article headlined "Keller Shows Work At Tucker Gallery," read:

"From such stuff as dreams are made of, Jon Louis [sic] Keller has woven a series of fantasies, from numbers 1

to 15...These paintings, plus a group of fascinatingly different ceramics, for the current exhibition.

"The ceramics consist of heads with hands, a deer's head, which the artist calls Albino, and ash trays with piquant quality.

"Many of the paintings are painted in a sea green tone, with weird, elongated figures introduced as if wandering through a lunar scene, recalling faintly the works of Salvador Dali."

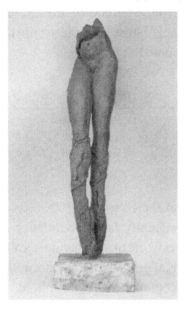 

After an absence of some years, with a dramatic movement of art from the blunt lines of the Depression to the abstract Post-Modernism that was capturing the imagination of the art world, for Keller to be described as recalling, however "faintly" the work of Dali, was heady praise indeed. The references to Dali would have particularly important to

Joan, who greatly admired his artistry, had embraced his style and was much enamored of the Dali School.

By August 1950, Keller appeared to be reclaiming her career. She had joined a newly formed select art group, founded in May, known as "The Seven", the only woman to be invited to join, and their first exhibit was to take place at the Tucker Gallery on August 11th, and run through the 25th. The show would feature everything from architectural scale models to surrealistic sculpture and oil paintings. Keller singled out in the press as the only female of the 'Select Seven' would be featuring her latest sculpture in the surrealistic fashion that had become the craze.

Eve Tucker Gallery

The Tucker Art Show in their "spic and span, cool looking" gallery drew a phenomenally large attendance of 500 guests to see the innovative work of the "avant-garde" of Miami's art world. It was Keller's work that drew the most attention and praise. Accompanied by a photo of distinctive upraised mounted hand, dubbed "The Hand", the press singled out Keller, writing "Joan Louie Keller's ceramics, one of whose bizarre pieces is here illustrated, have lost none of their fascination." At the same time, a "fantastic" (to quote the Miami News' Nellie Bower) painting by Keller was being showcased in the window of the Delius Gallery on 57 Street in New York City , which at the same time was featuring Old Master works by such notables as Fragonard and Tiepolo.

JOAN KELLER

At the end of January 1951, Joan, now consistently referred to as Jon Louie (or, incorrectly, as Jon Louis) Keller, announced she was opening her new school and sculpture and ceramic art at her studio, located at 645 West Flagler Street (no longer standing) on February 2nd. Well known and highly regarded for her unusual ceramic masks and figures, her work would continue to be handled by Eve Tucker's Galleries. Her new school was designed to be the gathering place for the many aspiring artists who, since her return, had expressed a wish to "study her unique style; beginners will receive instruction from her assistant."

Joan, together with two other Eve Tucker favorites – Robert Draper and Sandy Shaw - were back at the Tucker Galleries on April 1951 for a three-man exhibit of paintings, sculpture and ceramics, with a special preview on April 6 and running through the 20th. While Draper's abstract paintings and Joan's surrealistic sculptures were already highly esteemed, it was Shaw's first exhibit of his expressionist work.

The exhibit was a tremendous hit, as Miami art-lovers turned out en masse for the four-hour preview. It was virtually impossible to move through the throng that crowded the galleries to capacity. Keller, reviews noted, was clearly the star of the show, as reporter Nellie Bower of the Miami News relayed:

"Ms. Keller's ceramic sculpture, in which she combines a foundation of coral rock in some instances with ceramic tiles, are becoming well-known and well-liked in this area. The artist herself is a charming, almost too modest

115

person, whose work, subtle and delicate as it is, is the product of strong emotion, or so one feels.

"Her extraordinary dramatic piece "The Heart in the Stone*" is one of the most unusual things she has done. Her* Horses Head *created with coral rock as its base is realistic yet fantastic and is difficult to forget. Illustrated is a proudly beautiful in blue ceramic "Of her bones are corals made." "Joan's ceramic sculptures are always in good taste and bizarre as they are, lend themselves as vital decorations to any scheme of décor."*

Professionally, the year following the April 1951 Tucker Galleries exhibit appears to be a quiet one. Joan may have been concentrating on her two children (although she does not appear to have been overwhelmingly maternal, especially as her children grew). It wasn't for a year that her work appeared in another exhibit, again at the Tucker Galleries. Reunited with fellow original members of the avant-garde "Select Seven" members Sandy Shaw and Robert Draper, the trio's work was previewed the last exhibition of the Tucker season on April 11th and ran through the 24th.

The Miami News' Nellie Bower, who had consistently been a staunch support of Joan, did not fail her when reviewing the exhibit. Headlined '*ULTRA MODERNS EXHIBIT AT EVE TUCKER GALLERIES"*, her report read in part:

"In approaching an exhibit such as was seen at last Friday's preview at the Eve Tucker Galleries, 3917 Alton Rd., consisting of the work by a trio of ultra-moderns, in behooves one to divest oneself of all vieux jeu leanings as

one enters a world of expressionism largely Freudian from its conception to its ultimate creation.

JLTRA MODERNS EXHIBIT
AT EVE TUCKER GALLERIES

By NELLIE BOWER

In approaching an exhibit such as was seen at last Friday's preview at the Eve Tucker Galleries, 3917 Alton Rd., consisting of the work by a trio of ultra moderns, it behooves one to divest oneself of all vieux jeu leanings as one enters a world of expressionism largely Freudian from its conception to its ultimate creation.

"WOMEN AND children first" being a well established custom, I'll deal first with the work of Jon Louie Keller, a very gifted young woman sculptor, whose fine academic training shows up in two heads, one, a portrait of Abe Steinberg, here illustrated, and the other a self-portrait in sculptured ceramic. Both are delicate, yet strong, beautifully modeled and glazed with a refinement achieved only by the greatest care and rarely seen in works of this kind.

Among the seven or eight pieces shown by Miss Keller, one at least has semi-classical lines, though it is completely surrealistic in interpretation. This is a reclining figure called "Resignation." Her more decorative masks, for which she is justly famous in this area, are not included in her exhibit, but, like her work or not, it is strikingly different, and most painstakingly designed, executed and finished.

SANDY SHAW, also exhibiting, is the Young Man from Texas, and he turns out a great deal of new work constantly. His paintings continue to show the strong influence of the proximity in Mexico in his formative years

ABE STEINBERG
Ceramic Portrait by Jon L. Keller

"Bull With Banderillos" directly attributable to this association, but his distorted forms also come from this source. A few slightly modified ones such as "Cool Ones" and "Still Life With Bottle" are less harrowing and therefore probably most

choose "Pinto" as being the most interesting.

One thing is evident, Sandy Shaw has a fund of strange stories to tell which he does vividly and unrestrainedly in his canvases whether it is in "Branding," "Pastoral 1934" a story of the drought, or "Who Pulls the Strings?"

REGARDING the round dozen paintings, oils and watercolors at least half of which are non-objective abstractions (what contradiction in terms!) by Robert Draper, the only possible criterion can be, how do they affect the individual?

Beauty, as we know, is in the eye of the beholder and for that matter so is good design, texture, tonal harmony, balance, rhythm and every other quality pertaining to art, judging by the standards or lack of them recognized today. Mr. Draper is a sincere and earnest painter who after experimenting with various styles, has decided that he finds self-expression in such careful planned work as "Lake of the Aztec Gods," a cool and pleasingly toned phantasy which would lend sparkle to a home in the modern decor; or "Night Birds" which recently won the Beattie prize for moderns at the Artists and Writers Breakfast.

Vague forms are discernible in "Nymph and Satyr" and "Flight of the Dragon" both emerging from a riot of color. The latter, Mr. Draper has explained, is the result of his deep interest in Chinese art, while several other of his pictures owe their being to his absorption

"'Women and children first'' being a well-established custom, I'll deal first with the work of Jon Louie Keller, a very gifted young woman sculptor, whose fine academic training shows up in two heads, one, a portrait of Abe Steinberg here illustrated, and the other a self-portrait in sculptured ceramic. Both are delicate, yet strong, beautifully modeled and glazed with a refinement achieved only by the greatest care and rarely seen in works of this kind.

"Among the seven or eight pieces shown by Miss Keller, one at least has semi-classical lines, though it is completely surrealistic in interpretation. This is a reclining figure called 'Resignation.' Her more decorative masks, for which she is justly famous in this area, are not included in her

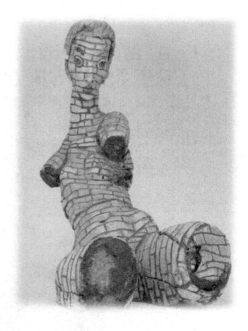

exhibit, but, like her work or not, it is strikingly different, and most painstakingly designed, executed and finished."

A July 6, 1952 news photo of a white ceramic portrait head and shoulders of Marian Voccaro, which had been her latest commission and was then on display at the Tucker Galleries, was the only mention of Keller that could be located. By February 1953, the Galleries had relocated to 1240 Lincoln Road, where a preview cocktail party was held for friends and clients for the three artists participating in the latest exhibition, featuring the work of Joan, Robert Draper and Don Gayer. Of Joan it was noted that her work in surrealist sculptures were well known both in Miami and Chicago, and that where she "has been spending her summers the last few years." No reference to her working or spending time in Chicago has been found, although family members do recall her doing so.

On March 1, 1953, Joan must have been blindsided when this latest exhibition earned her the first negative reviews of her career, and all the more so in that it came from the pen of the influential Miami News Arts Editor Nellie Bower, who had been a staunch advocate of Joan's work since her return from New York. While singing the praises of her co-exhibitionists Robert Draper and Don Gayer, the latter of whom who was apparently Bower's newest favorite, Bower dipped her pen in gentle, but unmistakable venom, when she turned on Keller.

"John Louis [sic] Keller, are well known both here and elsewhere, excels in so many facets of her work, her skillful modeling, the exquisitely thin and even glazes, her delicacy of handling, that I am loathe to go on record that my admiration for this fine little artist is not wholehearted. Yet I feel that the time has come that some reference must be made to the boredom which mounts as you see each modeled head either crownless or in some other way defaced. What offered a certain amount of novelty and interest several years ago, now has become somewhat monotonous.

"I believe that Jon Keller is to fine an artist to have become typed to the extent that she has. I liked best her very able watercolor sketches, Miss Tucker's portrait in ceramics, which captures the fine frankness of the subject, and "Song of Belitus" which combines clay with driftwood in a very interesting manner."

Cypress and Stone

"Belitus" it is clearly the same as 'Bilitis' produced by renowned French poet, writer, and gay rights champion Pierre Louys (1870-1925). Published as "Songs of Bilitis" in 1894, an erotic collection of 143 poems which expressed a pagan sensuality with stylistic perfection. The erotic work has an erotic lesbian, or female sexuality theme. "Songs of Bilitis" was said to have actually been written by the ancient Greek lyrical poetess Sappho, a Greek courtesan and lesbian poet from the island of Lesbos. At the time of the supposed discovery of this collection of erotic poems, it was believed a new literary masterpiece had been uncovered. In truth, it was the flamboyant Louys himself who had written it – "Bilitus" only existed in the world of sophisticated erotica. In 1926 the first illustrated edition, with drawings by Will Pogany and translated into English by Alvah C. Bessie, had a run of 2000 copies, which were privately printed for subscribers. It seems likely Joan's work was inspired in part by this essentially modern work.

Songs of Bilitus

This criticism Joan had taken did not deter Eve Tucker the following October, when her galleries were scheduled to reopen after a month's closing, to participate in Art Week, with a one-woman show of caseins (a paint derived from milk protein) and watercolors. The show hung from November 2nd through November 15th. In announcing the show, it was noted that though Joan was better known for her surrealistic sculpture, her paintings had gained her a sizeable following of collectors and admirers.

The exhibit consisted of some 16 drawings, and once again Nellie Bowers, who it should be remembered was an influential doyenne and critic of the Florida art world, dipped her pen in criticism. Bowers noted that of the 16 drawings,

> *"...some heightened with color, green predominating. They are completely surrealistic in feeling and subject and those who like Miss Keller's work will be able to admire here a rather complete range. Personally, though I like the delicacy of her touch and even her technique, in portraying figures, strange wispy trees, torsos, centaurs and even heads, all could be drift-wood in its many convolutions and this fact I found disagreeable."*

In April 1954, Nellie Bower once again homed in on Keller in a review of the exhibits on display in three different galleries, including Eve Tucker's. In discussing the three-man exhibit there (the others being Don Gayer and newcomer Clark Fiers, she acidly commented that Joan's drawings and sculpture "are such stuff as dreams are made of, not by any means happy ones for the most part." Bower went on:

> *"Don Gayer's strange shapes in every hue overshadow the more delicate but also more macabre work of Miss Keller. The poorly titled "Nocturne" done in a new medium – sculpture metal – is an extremely attenuated figure, which to several people who saw it, recalled a praying mantis. The fineness of her modeling and glazing, as for instance in "Ultimatum", also her driftwood and terra-cotta plaque – "Song Offering" counterbalance to some extent the less likable qualities. But more and more, she seems to draw inspiration from Dali in his earlier and more dreadful moments..."*

That Joan was enamored of the surrealist work was undeniable and influenced her own work. She painted portraits of her young children, Marie and Kenneth, in an obvious Daliesque style. Marie's portrait featured a broken doll and Marie's head was depicted as emerging from a decaying tree. Her son's portrait will be discussed in greater detail below.

Multiple disparaging reviews may have dampened Joan's ambition to create, but her increasingly abstract and, some said, bizarre, work no doubt also played a significant role in the noticeable decrease in her artistic prominence. The only mention of her in all of 1955 was when, after submitting two watercolors for display, she was merely mentioned for surrealistic bust entitled "Well of Loneliness." The event was held by the First Sunshine Festival Painting and Sculpture Exhibition, sponsored by the Creative Arts Group, located in the Tampa Bay area. The exhibition then went on display at the Contemporary Arts Gallery in Pinellas Park

Despite her career stalling Joan appeared, at least to her family, to be reasonably content with her life. One relative recalled she possessed a sizeable collection of art books and had a habit of using dollar bills to mark her place. Her reasoning for this was, to her, simple: *"I'll surely go back to finish my reading since there was a dollar there, and if I don't it will be like newfound money one day!"*. After her death, several of her books were found to still have that "newfound money" in them waiting to be reclaimed.

4302 Ingrham Highway

By this time, Joan, King Louie and their children had moved into a charming, if perhaps somewhat overgrown, home at 4302 Ingraham Highway in Coconut Grove, which at present is still standing. As Joan never drove a car, she used public transportation, which in the Grove entailed lengthy walks to the closest bus stops. On several of these walks, she would come across various animals which had been killed in the winding roadways and would carry their remains back to the Ingraham house for a dignified burial. Always an animal lover, Joan was particularly fonds of cats, and relatives remembered her home was almost overrun with felines at any given time.

Relatives also later recalled Joan's insatiable love of Coca-Cola. She invariably carried a large purse (one family member described them as more akin to a shopping bag. In it could be found some of her art supplies, groceries, possibly a carefully wrapped dead animal headed for burial, and always a couple of 8-ounce bottles of Coca Cola. It was not unusual to observe Joan entering one of the numerous diners and coffee shops that proliferated in downtown Miami, ask for a glass of ice, reach into her cavernous purse, extract a bottle of Coke and a bottle opener and proceed to pour her own refreshment.

Keller, Her Mother and Her Sister, Margaret

By 1956 it seemed Joan was becoming increasingly irrelevant to the modern art world. It had become the era of high school sock-hops, "I Love Lucy" dominating the television, bigger cars, bigger homes and comfortable suburbs. For Joan, a survivor of the Great Depression, it was a new world, little of which she was likely to relate. A display of her work in February that year by the loyal Eve Tucker was dismissed by the increasingly deprecating Nellie Bower:

"With the passing of time, it seems to me that Jon Keller's sculpture, which is made up of ceramic clay, metal,

coral rock and many other combinations, becomes more and more bizarre.

"Her present display at Eve Tucker's place on Lincoln Road is comprised of some new and some pieces of sculpture, also a number of caseins [caseins are an emulsion made from a solution of a protein precipitated by milk, water and ammonia carbonate]. *Nearly all have a most ghastly appearance."*

It would be two years before Joan and her work returned to the Tucker Galleries on January 18, 1958, in what would prove to be her final exhibit there. This was a joint exhibition with painter Arthur Voelkel. After several years of criticizing and dismissing Joan's work, for this exhibit the press, especially Nellie Bower, tossed bouquets of compliments. Under the headline *"Delicacy, Fine Glaze and Feeling Characterize Jon Keller Portraits,"* the review read in part:

"When Jon Keller sticks to straight portraiture in ceramic sculpture, the result is nothing short of exquisite.

"The few pieces she is showing at the Eve Tucker Galleries mark her as an artist of premier rank: for here's delicate modeling, fine thin even glaze and a wealth of feeling.

"Her drawings into which she introduces figures also have much to recommend them, notably that entitled 'Artist's Daughter.'

"A true friend would hit her over the head when she takes up her tools to do any more of those lamentably Freudian pieces – those gargoyles and holes-in-the-head figures.

"Her latest portrait series – that of Mrs. Hank Meyer and her two children proclaim her as a top-notch artist in a field not too frequently attempted by women; also in this class is a head of Stephen Kern, son of Mr. and Mrs. Jerome Kern."

And with that fulsome, undiluted praise, almost a forgiveness to a wayward child who has come to their senses, no more was heard about Joan…until the end.

Meyers Family Sculpture, 1958

SCULPTRESS FORGOTTEN

CHAPTER 8
ENDINGS – MIAMI &
RHODE ISLAND
1960-1963

ENDINGS – MIAMI & RHODE ISLAND 1960-1963

Sometime around 1960, Joan's mother asked her to do a religious painting for her, a request with which Joan complied. Presented to her as a birthday present, "Mary, Queen of Heaven" featured the elongated hands and neck typical of her work. It was unsigned, again not unusual for her. During the late 1950s and into the early 1960s, Joan executed murals for several restaurants and clubs in the Miami area, but her years of exhibits and showings were pretty much a thing of much treasured past.

By 1961, King Louie, Joan's husband for some 16 years, had for some time been the co-owner/partner of the Aloha Restaurant, which specialized in Asian cuisine. Located in Coral Gables at 3727 SW 8 Street (near the intersection of Douglas Road and SW 8 Street; the building is no longer standing), it had been a popular eatery for some years. Joan, King and their two children were still living on Ingraham Highway. Family life with Joan, while perhaps a bit eccentric, was apparently peaceful and uneventful.

Matchbook from King Louie's Restaurant, the Aloha

Everything changed in the early hours of December 23, 1961. Christmas was two days away, and two major football games, a sport dear to the heart of Miamians, were imminent. The North-South game, always a favorite, was to be played on Christmas Day, pitting the best of the 'Yankee' college teams' players against the South's finest. The Orange Bowl game, which, along with the Sugar Bowl and the Sun Bowl, was among the the second oldest bowl games in the country, was ready to rumble on New Year's Day. Between these two major sports events and the holidays, Miami was filled to overflowing with out-of-town visitors and fans.

Shortly before 1:00 AM on December 23, Louie left the Aloha and was headed home to Coconut Grove when he was involved in a minor auto accident at the intersection of Bird Road and SW 58 Avenue. It was little more than a fender-bender with another car, driven by Thomas Jackson, 39, from Rushton, Louisiana. No one was injured and Louie stepped out of his car to retrieve a piece of debris from the accident, possibly part of a fender. It was then, at 1:05 AM, that a third car appeared, driven by a possibly intoxicated 20-year-old Jerome Groane, of 3700 SW 88 Place. Groane plowed into Louie. Critically injured, Louie was rushed to South Miami Hospital. It would later be speculated that Joan was in Louie's car when the tragedy occurred.

Louie (whose race was listed as "yellow") lingered on past Christmas before dying at 10:30 on the morning of December 26th. The cause of death was listed as bronchopneumonia, multiple fractures, and epidural hematoma. Joan, who signed the death certificate as Mrs. Jon Louie, stated they lived at 4302 Ingraham Highway. Funeral services were held at the Combs Coral Gables Chapel at 1661 Douglas Road. Louie was buried at sea the following day. He was 44 years old.

Dade Man Killed;
Traffic Toll 137

Dade County's traffic fatal-
total rose to 137 Tuesday
th the death of King Louie,
year-old Chinese - American,
4302 Ingram Highway, Cor-
Gables. Louie died at South
iami Hospital.

A Metro Police accident In-
stigator said that Louie was
ruck at 1:05 a.m. on Dec.
at Bird Rd. and SW 58th
ve. in the strange aftermath
a previous accident.

Louie's car figured in a minor
llision with another car driv-
by Thomas Jackson, 39, of
iston, La. When Louie got
t of his car and stooped to
ck up a piece of debris from
e pavement, he was hit by
other vehicle, driven by 20-
ar-old Jerry Groane, of 3700
W 8S TH

Counry's traffic fatality numb
stood at 150.

King Louie

Services for King Louie, 44, of 4302
Ingraham Highway, who died Tuesday,
will be at 10 a.m. Friday in Combs
Coral Gables Chapel. He came here 12
years ago from New York City and was
a partner in the Aloha Restaurant in
Coral Gables. Surviving are his wife,
Jon; a daughter, Marie; and a son,
Kenneth, all of Miami.

As the shock of her husband's death began to wane, Joan resumed working, but with much less enthusiasm or public notice that she enjoyed in the past. It is possible that at some point around this time she may have left the Ingraham home and moved to 96 West 1st Street, a property which could not be identified on any current maps.

Joan often visited her sister Julia at the hotel-rooming house, near Hialeah Racetrack, which had belonged to Julia since her husband Cyril's death. Julia, who hand endured an abusive marriage of nearly 12 years to the alcoholic Vince Gillen (with whom she had two children, Joseph Vincent and Julia), finally had enough and divorced him in May 1962.

While it is speculation on the part of her family, it may have been at the track that Joan met a man, of whom relatively little is known, and what is known is not particularly flattering.

Theodore (Woody) Wojcik (occasionally spelled Wotcik) was said to be a regular at Hialeah Racetrack. During its glamorous heyday, it hosted such luminaries at Presidents Truman, Kennedy and Nixon, as well as such stars and celebrities as Sinatra, Crosby, Jolson, the Duke and Duchess of Windsor, Princess Grace of Monaco (also known as film star Grace Kelly), Glenn Ford, Elizabeth Taylor and scores of others. Wojick seemingly thrived on rubbing shoulders with the elite – implying he was a wealthy high-roller of impeccable old-guard stock.

Wojcik's background was actually far more modest. He was born in Central Falls, Providence County, Rhode Island (a far cry from the toney Newport). How he made his way to Miami and would meet Joan is unknown. What is known is that her family looked askance at him from the moment they met him. Despite the wariness of her family and friends, Joan and Woody married in April 1963, just 16 months after King Louie's death.

Just before Joan and Wojick married, the matriarch on the Keller family, Marie Frances Roach Keller Bernier, who lived with Julia, died on April 3. She was survived by her three daughters, and her body was taken back to Cleveland and buried beside her second husband Joseph Bernier (who had died 32 years before) at Calvary Cemetery. Her death left her eldest daughter Julia Keller Brickman Gillen the de facto matriarch of the Keller family.

Woody Wojick was the son of James and Anna Gadomski Wojick. He was probably born October 19, 1924 (per the Social Security Index), but other dates range from 1920 (noted in a brief obituary), September 11, 1923 (his Social Security application) and September 19, 1924 (the US

Department of Veteran Affairs BIRLS Death file). In September 1940, his last name was given as Wotcik (with "Wojick" noted in parentheses), but by 1942 was spelled Wojick, the surname he continued to use. He was still living in Providence in 1949. In 1955 he traveled to Cuba, most likely on a gambling junket to that freewheeling island 90 miles from Florida's southernmost shores.

Whether it shortly before or after Joan met Wojick, she resumed actively pursuing her artistic career. Never noted for her maternal instincts, Joan left her 12-year-old son Kenny with friends (her daughter Marie had moved, at age 17, across the country to Long Beach, CA). When Joan did not return to pick up Kenny, he was handed over to the authorities. He managed to slip away from their custody but was soon located at the Orange Bowl Stadium. Julia heard of what had transpired and retrieved Kenny, and he would subsequently live with her permanently. Very fond of his aunt, he soon took to calling her "Mom."

It was around this time that Joan received one of her last commissions – and it was a major one at that. Miami Beach's newest luxury hotel, the Doral Beach, and their club, the Doral Country Club, retained her top two 13-foot statues for the hotel. According to some printed reports, they were never completed, while other contemporaries state they were finished, but were damaged at some later date by a hurricane. They were subsequently either disposed of or put in storage. A member of the Keller family later visited the hotel to see the statues, only to be told they had been broken up and unceremoniously dumped into the Atlantic Ocean.

According to family members, it was while Joan was working on these statues that "her eyes went bad." Wojick, for reasons that remain unclear, chose to take Joan back to his native Rhode Island "for doctors' eye care there." Perhaps it was Providence's proximity to major hospitals in the Boston area, 50 miles away. Some relatives believed it was Joan who requested to be taken to Providence, others felt there were other unknown reasons on the part of Wojick. The answer will never be known, but Joan would find herself in the wrong place at the wrong time.

Keller by Candlelight

"FAMED GROVE ARTIST MODEL DIES AT RHODE ISLAND RETREAT" read one of the several headlines announcing Joan had been found dead on August 13th. According to one report, Joan was alone in the Providence house when she collapsed in the bathroom, striking her head. Her body was taken to Boston for an autopsy, but despite numerous attempts, as of this writing,

neither her death certificate nor autopsy report have been made available. Rhode Island authorities have told family members that many of these records are only retained for 25 years, so they may no longer exist.

Some members of her family were, and remain, suspicious of what actually caused her death from her fall, arguing that while she may have injured her head, was that what actually killed her? On face value it is a legitimate question. Other sources have said that Joan was found drowned in a full bathtub, and that her sister Julia demanded, and received a police photograph confirming that. No one living today has claimed to have seen such a photo. In any event, it would not prove whether her drowning was an accident, a suicide or something else.

When Julia was notified of Joan's death, she immediately made plans to fly north to handle the funeral arrangements, only to be informed they had already been made. Joan, an artist endowed with a rare combination of ethereal physical beauty and a great talent, especially in the rugged sort of sculpting at which she excelled, was buried at sea, 13 miles off the Rhode Island coast on August 16th, leaving more questions than answers.

Joan was survived by her daughter Marie, son Kenny, who had turned 13 two months earlier and was living with Julia, and her two sisters, Julia, and Margaret, both of Hialeah. Interestingly, only one report on her death mentioned her widower. Whether the omission was an oversight or deliberate remains unknown.

CHAPTER 9

THE SURVIVORS, 1963 – 1996

THE SURVIVORS, 1963 – 1996

Joan left a number of surviving family members at the time of her unexpected death. It was a family that had endured their fair share of unusual and tragic events, and after Joan, it would continue. As this book has dealt extensively with her family, a brief look at their lives after Joan is in order.

Joan's eldest sister, Julia. Widowed by Cyril Brickman, and divorced from Vince Gillen in 1962, endured local headlines two years later. In the early morning hours of January 26, 1964, an intoxicated Vince Gillen, then 50, broke into the home of his girlfriend, a south Dade beautician, Mrs. Jewel Brown at her house, located in a peaceful, rural subdivision, at the rear of an estate at 6919 SW 101 Street.

Unfortunately, Mrs. Brown's ex-husband, Jess Brown was there. Gillen had arrived at the house around midnight and attempted to break the door down. Unsuccessful, he was persuaded to leave by a friend, who drove him off. Gillen, still intoxicated and furious, returned to the house by cab around 3:00 AM. This time he was successful in breaking in. Wielding a butcher knife and a paring knife, he attacked Jess Brown, who himself grabbed a butcher knife from the kitchen.

In the melee, Brown sustained only a superficial knife wound to his right arm. Gillen was not as fortunate. Brown inflicted two stab wounds near Gillen's heart and three more in his neck. Gillen died at the scene – but according to authorities, not from the wounds. His autopsy states he succumbed to acute alcoholism, with his alcohol level at death of .386. Police said they had no address for Gillen, only that he had worked at Tropical Race Park and had recently been employed putting up campaign posters for Metro Commission candidates. His body was identified by Julia on the morning of his death. His brief obituary referred to him as "of Tropical Race Park." A rosary was held at the Carl F. Slade Hialeah-Miami Springs Funeral Home. Gillen was buried in Section A of Woodlawn Park, not far from the grave of Julia's first husband.

This was essentially the version of Gillen's death that was reported by the press. His autopsy report, while in accord with some of what was printed, contained information that raise some questions. While this is a story for another book, police reports stated that the weapons, used by both men, consisted of a 3" paring knife, a carving knife with an 8 ½ " blade, and a butcher knife with a 7" blade. The autopsy report referred to Gillen as well-nourished and well-developed (although his weight was only 140 pounds). They noted nine, not five, traumatic injuries, ranging from his chest, his back and arm, noting that all but two were considered superficial.

Curiously, Jewel Brown and her ex-husband left her house by car, to locate a policeman, returning about 3:45 AM. For such an altercation, one would think the death scene would have been in some disarray, but there was little evidence of any disturbance. To say the least, it is curious that Gillen sustained nine noted knife wounds, at least two of which were serious, yet he died of alcohol poisoning.

As for Julia, she would live most of the rest of her life in Hialeah and adjacent Miami Springs. Only 51 when Vince Gillen died, she never remarried and died in Miami on February 10, 1993, Julia was buried beside her first husband, Cyril Brickman, who had died 47 years before. It will be recalled that it was Brickman, together with Julia's brother John Keller, who led the Keller family's move from Cleveland to Miami.

Margaret Keller McGuire, the youngest of the Keller sisters, and her husband James were long-time residents of New York City. Once a beautiful woman, she sadly developed a form of mental illness that grew increasingly worse. Her sickness deteriorated to the point that her husband simply wanted nothing more to do with Margaret and sent her to Miami for her sister to deal with. She lived with Julia for a time before her condition forced Julia to have admitted to the Florida State Hospital in Broward County, where she died at the age of 47 on August 22, 1967. Her estranged husband, who was several years her senior, died five years later, on February 11, 1972.

John Keller, the only son in the family, who had been killed during WWII, left behind his wife Rhoda and a son, John E. Keller. Rhoda eventually remarried, to Andrew D. Snoke of Ohio. The couple eventually moved to Sebastian, Indian River, FL. Snoke, who was born December 21, 1917, died there August 4, 2002. Rhoda, continued to live in Sebastian until her death, the last surviving member of the Keller siblings and their assorted spouses. She was survived by her son John.

Of Joan's two children, Marie, said to be just as beautiful as her mother, had headed to California when she was 17 and initially living in Long Beach and Los Angeles. It has been said she aspired to become a film actress. Marie had the beauty, and possibly talent, but it was bad timing. The early 1960s, were the waning years of "Golden Age" of Hollywood, as the once mighty studio system weakened. The era of grooming potential stars who were under coveted seven-year studio contracts, was rapidly coming to an end. The number of films being released was dropping quickly. Television had captured a public who had for decades gone to the movies at least once a week. Marie's middle name, which she adopted when she was around 20, was Lansang, telling family members it derived from her father being a native of China.

Marie Louie

When she arrived in 1963, panic had hit the industry and a new crop of powerful agents arrived, making the chances of an unknown like Marie getting a break unlikely. By 1966 she was living at 1310 Las Palmas and employed as a gardener at 4340 Llano Drive. At some point she was employed by the Howard Hughes' organization, possibly at his Romaine Street headquarters in Los Angeles.

On October 20, 1967, the 21-year-old Marie Louie married Hidenobu Iwawaki, of Japanese origin, in Los Angeles. Iwawaki was several years her senior, being born in 1931. The marriage was brief and childless, ending in a January 1970 divorce. Iwawaki died in 2004. Marie, who never remarried, remained in California, living at such various addresses as 2607 Alsace Avenue, Los Angeles and 830 Tuscany Avenue, Venice, CA (both 1984), and 635 Whiting Street in El Segundo (1993). By 1997, Marie had moved to Port Townsend, WA, living there until her death on February 19, 2008.

Joan's son Kenneth endured a somewhat challenging adolescence. His aunt Julia was said to have adopted him, although it was apparently an informal arrangement. After high school, he attended St. John Vianney Seminary in Westchester, studied at Miami-Dade Community College's North Campus and graduated from the University of Florida Dental School in Gainesville. He remained there, serving on the faculty of the College of Dentistry before going on to earn his master's degree from St. Louis University. While in St. Louis, he was honored with the Milo Hellman Award for his work in dental research. In 1984, Kenneth returned to Miami, where he opened a successful dental practice in Miami Lakes.

In addition to his thriving practice, Kenneth was an avid volunteer coach for the Optimists Club baseball team. Extremely popular for his both his work and his community involvement, it came as a shock when Kenneth was diagnosed with cancer. The prognosis was grim, and he died on October 13, 1989 at the young age of 39.

"Kenneth was a very caring and patient person," said his cousin George "Guy" Brickman. "Parents brought their children to him were happy because he always took the time to explain everything to them. And the kids he worked with just loved him." In addition to his beloved aunt Julia and sister Marie, he was survived by his cousins Jack, Bill Pat, Guy and Mike Brickman, Joe Gillen and

Keller Portrait of her Son, Kenneth

Julie Gillen Evans, all of whom were Julia's children. Following a visitation at the Van Orsdel North Miami Chapel, followed the next day by Burial Mass at Our Lady of the Lakes Catholic Church. He was buried at Woodlawn Park, adjacent to his late uncle Cyril Brickman, and where Julia would be laid to rest a few years later.

In addition to his aunt and cousins, Kenneth was survived by Dr. John Reville, his closest and dearest friend.

It was a friendship that dated back to their school days. It was to Reville that Kenneth made the request that, like both his parents, he be buried at sea. He also gifted Reville with the Daliesque portrait Joan had done of him as a child. The painting has always had a special meaning to Reville and continues to occupy a prominent place in his Houston home.

This now brings us to the last, most mysterious and, as some would venture to opine, sinister survivor of this story – Joan's second husband, Theodore "Woody" Wojick. As mentioned above, his date of birth has been noted as early as 1920 and as late as 1924. His one-line obituary gave his age as 76, but he was probably closer to 72. The only constant is that he was born in Central Falls, RI. If this was simply sloppy recording, it was extensive,

Wojick was a serious gambler, albeit without a serious bankroll to fund his wagering. When he met Joan, it is possible he would think that a well-known artist and Conover model, whose recent husband had been a partner in a popular restaurant, and who lived in Coconut Grove should be someone he should get to know better…or maybe the brief courtship was simply an honest one.

The questions surrounding Wojick's taking Joan to Rhode Island for medical treatment are several, and now, almost 60 years later, will remain unanswered. The couple had been wed less than five months, and all of Joan's family were in Miami. A slip in a bathroom resulting in death is possible, but not common. What of the photograph Julia demanded, showing Joan dead in a bathtub? What prompted such hasty arrangements for a burial at sea? It was only natural that Joan's family had reservations about the events that caused her death.

Wojick and the Keller family did not have any relationship after Joan's death, although he did return to Miami and lived in Hialeah. Still a gambler, he made headlines on March 11, 1964, eight months after his wife's death, when he hit a twin double at Hialeah Racetrack, winning over $21,000 (the equivalent of over $175,000 in 2020). Wojick, identified in the press as "of Central Falls, Rhode Island," insisted on collecting his windfall in cash.

After that lucky day, Wojick dropped from sight. Whether he remarried is unknown. At his death, Wojick was a resident of Hialeah. While no obituary could be found in the Miami press, a one-line obituary appeared in the Palm Beach Post:

"THEODORE WOJICK, 76, of Hialeah died March 6, 1996." Why his death went unnoticed in Miami, but was noted in Palm Beach, submitted by a Boynton Beach funeral home, is yet another question unanswered.

AFTERWORD

SCULPTRESS FORGOTTEN

AFTERWORD

Despite best efforts, there remain several questions regarding Joan Keller. Among them are what prompted her temporary abandonment of her promising career in art and changing her change of profession to a glamorous cover girl? What prompted Joan to leave Miami and move to New York? What were the reasons behind her apparent lack of maternal instincts, particularly after her first husband's untimely death? What was the full story behind her death at the age of 46? We will never have all the answers, but in chronicling a person's life, it's unlikely anyone would have all the answers.

What we can state is what we do know. We know a girl whose father died when she was a mere infant...a teenager during the 1920s when that decade was roaring at its loudest...watching as her family tried to survive the Great Depression in Cleveland, one of the hardest hit in the country...moving with her family to Miami when she was 18 and discovering her innate talent of transforming a piece of rock into a masterful work of art...a beautiful young lady becoming one of the WPA's most noted artists in just three years...becoming the Cinderella Girl of Florida's art world, her work being showcased at the New York World's Fair...the abrupt change of gears and becoming a popular model in the competitive world of Manhattan, gracing the glossy pages of such magazines as Vogue...returning to Miami and more acclaim as she expanded her art...her eccentricities of removing dead animals off local roads and putting them in her purse for proper burial...her use of dollar bills for bookmarks...her first husband's sudden death...and then her own sudden demise that has yet to be fully understood. This was the Joan Keller whose stone "Fireman" have become on the most iconic images of Coral Gables.

This is the Joan Keller who deserves to be remembered. Let her also represent the scores of local artists during the Great Depression, many tremendously talented, others less so, but all of whom took their work seriously and passionately. While mostly forgotten today, these young artists deserve to be remembered, in the context of their time and place. Joan Keller is their symbolic figurehead. We hope we have done her justice.

Margaret and Jon "Tess" Keller
New York City
Circa 1940's

Joan Theresa "Tess" Keller

1916 – 1963

Made in the USA
Middletown, DE
09 February 2021